An Introduction to
The Urantia Revelation

by David Bradley

An Introduction to the Urantia Revelation

First Edition 1998
Second Edition 2002
©1998, 2002 David Bradley

Published by:
White Egret Publications
251 F Street
Arcata, CA 95521

(707) 822-2577

All rights reserved. No part of this work may be reproduced or transmitted in any form or by any means, electronic or mechanical, including photocopying or recording, or by any information storage or retrieval system, without permission in writing from the publisher or author, except for brief quotations embodied in critical articles or reviews.

This document contains quotes from *The URANTIA Book*, which was copyrighted in 1955 © by URANTIA Foundation; 533 Diversey Parkway; Chicago, Illinois 60614; 773-525-3319, all rights reserved. The author is using these quotes by permission from URANTIA Foundation, which owns the copyright. Any interpretations, opinions, or conclusions — whether stated or implied — are those of the author and may not represent the views of URANTIA Foundation or its affiliates.

Author's Note, January 2002: I understand the URANTIA Foundation no longer holds the copyright but may regain it upon appeal. For purposes of this book, I am assuming they do hold it.

Library of Congress Catalog Card Number: 98-92687
ISBN 0-9663270-1-2
Printed in the United States of America
March, 2002

Author's Preface:

My goal is to present an introduction to the basic concepts contained in *The Urantia Book*, along with examples of its teachings and viewpoints. Except for basic concepts, I have included only a small and selective fraction of the wealth of information and teachings contained in *The Urantia Book*. My selection of example topics and quotations is surely biased by my own point of view and interests.

I greatly enjoy the book and its concepts, and this introduction became longer than I originally intended. Therefore, I begin with an introductory chapter that provides an overview, and a summary of basic conclusions or meanings.

There are many new concepts in *The Urantia Book*. To avoid repeated explanations, I have included a glossary for reference.

I would like to thank Don for launching the idea, and Laurie, Matthew, and others for helpful reviews. Comments from readers are greatly appreciated.

About Quotes:

All quotes herein are from *The Urantia Book*, as published by The Urantia Foundation, fourth printing, 1973. I have indexed each quote by including the Paper, Section, Paragraph, and Page numbers. The indexing locates the beginning of the quote. For example: P23,S3,PP4,PG261 translates to "Paper 23, Section 3, Paragraph 4, Page 261".

Where the section number is omitted, the text appears at the beginning of the paper, before Section 1. Where the section number is a roman numeral, it is from *The Urantia Book*'s Foreword.

Some quotes I use are full paragraphs, and some are selected sentences, partial sentences, or partial paragraphs. Three dots ... are shown where I have omitted text, which may be words omitted from a sentence, or sentences omitted from a paragraph. Where I added comments to help explain a quote, my comments are in brackets [ ].

Table of Contents

	Page
Author's Preface	i
CHAPTER 1: BRIEF INTRODUCTION AND OVERVIEW	1
CHAPTER 2: *THE URANTIA BOOK* - WHAT IS IT? WHO WROTE IT?	5
CHAPTER 3: CREATOR, CREATION, AND COSMOLOGY	9
CHAPTER 4: PLANETARY HISTORY AND DISPENSATIONS	15
a. Introduction	15
b. The Planetary Prince	17
c. The Material Son and Daughter	19
d. The Magisterial Son	21
e. The Bestowal Son	22
f. The Trinity Teacher Sons	24
g. What Happened Here on Earth	24
CHAPTER 5: THE LUCIFER REBELLION, AND ADAM AND EVE'S DEFAULT	27
a. The Lucifer Rebellion in our Local System	27
b. The Rebellion on our Planet, and Some More Planetary History	28
c. Adam and Eve's Default	31
d. A Positive Result of the Rebellion and the Default	34
CHAPTER 6: WOMEN, MEN, EQUALITY, MARRIAGE, AND FAMILY	35
a. Feminine Attributes of God	35
b. Men, Women, and Equality	36
c. Marriage and Family	38
CHAPTER 7: RELIGION	41
a. Types of Religion	41
b. Religions of Authority/Religions of Spirit	42
c. Erroneous Scripture Concepts	43
d. Science, Secularism, Mechanistic Universe	45
e. Social Religious Potential	46
f. Religion and the Individual	47
g. Prayer and Worship	48
CHAPTER 8: SELECTED TOPICS	49
a. Cosmic Properties	49
b. Matter and Energy; Undiscovered Energy	50
c. Suggestions for Living	51

	d.	More Historic Notes	53
	e.	Equality, Race, Biologic Inheritance	54
	f.	War	55
	g.	Government, Civilization	58
	h.	Nature	60
	i.	Spirit and Flesh	60
	j.	Finding Eden	61
	k.	Food for Thought	62

CHAPTER 9: GOVERNMENT ON A NEIGHBORING PLANET — 63

	a.	The Continental Nation	63
	b.	Political Organization	64
	c.	The Home Life	64
	d.	The Educational System	65
	e.	Industrial Organization	65
	f.	Old-age Insurance	66
	g.	Taxation	66
	h.	The Special Colleges	67
	i.	The Plan of Universal Suffrage	67
	j.	Dealing With Crime	67
	k.	Military Preparedness	68
	l.	The Other Nations	68

CHAPTER 10: SPIRITUAL MINISTRIES TO HUMANS — 69

	a.	The Indwelling Fragment of God, the Thought Adjuster or Mystery Monitor	70
	b.	The Holy Spirit of the Local Universe Divine Minister or Mother Spirit	71
	c.	The Seven Adjutant Mind-spirits Bestowed by the Local Universe Divine Minister or Mother Spirit	71
	d.	Our Local Universe Creator Son and his Bestowed Spirit of Truth	72
	e.	Seraphic Ministries (Angels)	73
	f.	Co-ordinated Ministry	74
	g.	Midwayers	74

CHAPTER 11: LIFE AFTER DEATH — 77

CHAPTER 12: WHO JESUS WAS, WHAT HE DID, AND EXCERPTS FROM HIS LIFE AND TEACHINGS — 83

	a.	Review	83
	b.	Additional Perspective	84
	c.	Announcements	86
	d.	Birth	87
	e.	Herod's Attempt	88
	f.	Family Life	88
	g.	Adult Life, Prior to Public Ministry	92
	h.	John the Baptist; the Beginning of Public Ministry	93
	i.	Examples of Jesus' Teachings and Attitudes	94

j.	Fruits of the Spirit	98
k.	Examples of Healings	99
l.	Miscellaneous Excerpts	100
m.	On Jesus' Promised Return	102
n.	Nearing the End of His Earth Life	102
o.	The Last Supper	103
p.	Last Moments of Freedom	104
q.	The Crucifixion	106
r.	The Resurrection	107
s.	Pentecost and the Bestowal of the Spirit of Truth	108
t.	Persecution	109
u.	The Fate of the Apostles	109

GLOSSARY   113

BOOK ORDER FORM   Follows Page 120

ILLUSTRATIONS

Figure 1 The Grand Universe (Inhabited) Map View	Follows Page 10
Figure 2 Sectional Views of the Grand and Master Universes	Follows Page 10
Administrative Center of Satania, Our Local System	On Page 78

CHAPTER 1: BRIEF INTRODUCTION AND OVERVIEW

God is love, the creator, sustainer, and upholder of all creation. *The Urantia Book* is a great revelation, a presentation of universal facts and truths to us, about the creator and about creation. It greatly expands our views and understandings of the creator and the cosmos, and with this bigger picture, science, religion, history, and other areas of human knowledge become integrated. We are not alone in the universe, quite the contrary. *The Urantia Book* was written by love-respecting, civilized inhabitants of the universe. It was written by a revelatory committee, initially through a contact human, for the betterment of our planet. The identity of the contact human is unknown and unimportant. Urantia is the name of our planet.

The Urantia Book revelation is not small; the edition quoted has 2,097 pages of fine print. For most of us, it is not a quick study or easy reading.

The Urantia Book is wonderful. It reveals a much larger perspective of the cosmos we live in, of God, and of universe inhabitants, than previously known here on Earth. Its revelations are presented in four parts.

Part 1, The Central and Superuniverses, is about God, God's relationship to creation, God's relationship to individuals, and the structure and inhabitants of the greater cosmos. Part 2, The Local Universe, is about our part of the cosmos. Topics include creation, evolution, administration, and inhabitants of the local universe. Part 3, The History of Urantia, includes information about the origin of our planet, and about physical, biological, social, and spiritual evolution. Part 4, The Life and Teachings of Jesus, is self-explanatory.

Let's begin with a two paragraph quote:

> "Your world, Urantia, is one of many similar inhabited planets which comprise the local universe of Nebadon. This universe, together with similar creations, makes up the superuniverse of Orvonton, from whose capital, Uversa, our commission hails. Orvonton is one of the seven evolutionary superuniverses of time and space which circle the never-beginning, never-ending creation of divine perfection — the central universe of Havona. At the heart of this eternal and central universe is the stationary Isle of Paradise, the geographic center of infinity and the dwelling place of the eternal God.
>
> The seven evolving superuniverses in association with the central and divine universe, we commonly refer to as the grand universe; these are the now organized and inhabited creations. They are all a part of the master universe, which also embraces the uninhabited but mobilizing universes of outer space." FOREWORD,PP5,PG1 [The

commission mentioned in this quote is, collectively, the author of the first section of *The Urantia Book*.]

As you can see, *The Urantia Book* introduces us to many new concepts, such as the "Isle of Paradise" mentioned above. There is, I believe, no easy way to prove the reality or truthfulness of *The Urantia Book*, other than by truth recognition, our ability to recognize and accept things that 'ring true' to us. Truth recognition has to do with God.

> "The recognition of *true relations* implies a mind competent to discriminate between truth and error. The bestowal Spirit of Truth which invests the human minds of Urantia is unerringly responsive to truth—the living spirit relationship of all things and all beings as they are co-ordinated in the eternal ascent Godward." P56,S10,PP10,PG647

Other than by truth recognition, credibility of *The Urantia Book* can be verified by comparing certain scientific and historic facts presented in *The Urantia Book* against observations that can be made here on Earth. For example, *The Urantia Book* discusses the geologic history of our planet, including continental drift, which can be checked against the existing planetary geologic record.

What does *The Urantia Book* ask of us? What are its "bottom lines"? The following are a summary of what are, in my opinion, some of the basic meanings, suggestions, and conclusions contained in *The Urantia Book* revelation:

- Love, love, and more love.

- Service to our fellow humans.

- God is for real, and God is good.

- God's attributes are good things such as love, loyalty, mercy, compassion, truth, power, beauty, justice, and goodness; not anger, vengefulness, and punishment.

- You will do well to seek, find, and follow God through your own personal experiences, rather than following religious rules, or religious authorities.

- You are not coerced, you are a "will creature". You are free to choose.

- God is a true and loving parent to every human being. All humans are brothers and sisters in this regard. This is the gospel that Jesus actually taught.

- "That which the world needs most to know is: Men are the sons of God, and through faith they can actually realize, and daily experience, this ennobling truth." P193,PP4,PG2052

- Your entry into the family of God (Kingdom of Heaven) is by God's eternal loving acceptance and mercy; the door is open.

- God asks of us to learn, grow, and progress, to "Be you perfect, even as I am perfect,..." P1,PP6,PG22. [But not overnight; more like a step at a time.]

- Through a long evolutionary process/struggle, our planet will someday become "settled in light and life" (go positive).

- A fragment of God, a spark of divinity, lives within each of us, guiding us Godward. "Every mortal who is consciously or unconsciously following the leading of his indwelling Adjuster is living in accordance with the will of God." P107,PP4,PG1176 [The Thought Adjuster or Mystery Monitor is that fragment of God that dwells within each of us.]

- There is life after death. If we do not reject God, our lives continue after we physically die. Our souls, along with our personalities, are what survive death. Our souls are created by our choices that are acceptable to, or in accordance with, the indwelling guidance of God.

- There is no hell; those that choose to reject God's ways are not punished forever, they are fairly and justly adjudicated, and if found to have no survival value, they are undone as personalities.

- "Modern men and women of intelligence evade the religion of Jesus because of their fears of what it will do to them—and with them. And all such fears are well founded. The religion of Jesus does, indeed, dominate and transform its believers, demanding that men dedicate their lives to seeking for a knowledge of the will of the Father in heaven and requiring that the energies of living be consecrated to the unselfish service of the brotherhood of man." P195,S9,PP6,PG2083

- "It is the very goodness of God that leads men into true and genuine repentance." P143,S2,PP7,PG1610

- The "...only possible gift of true value to the Paradise Father..." is the "...affectionate dedication of the human will to the doing of the Father's will..." P1,S1,PP2,PG22, and, *The Urantia Book* suggests we positively affirm that "It is my will that your will be done." P111,S5,PP6,PG1221

The Urantia Book is generally written in male oriented language, which I believe reflects social customs of the time in which it was written. For example, usages such as man, mankind, The Fatherhood of God, and the Brotherhood of Man are common (see the three quotes immediately above). However, *The Urantia Book*, as Jesus did, asserts the equality of women and men. For example:

> "The apostles were at first shocked by, but early became accustomed to, Jesus' treatment of women; he made it very clear to them that women were to be accorded equal rights with men in the kingdom." P138,S8,PP8,PG1546

> "We do not regard a planet as having emerged from barbarism as long as one sex seeks to tyrannize over the other." P49,S4,PP4,PG564

The book reveals feminine attributes of God, as well as masculine. For example, consider that our local universe (which contains approximately ten million inhabited planets) is named Nebadon, and that Salvington is its headquarters sphere, then:

> "At the head of all personality in Nebadon stands the Creator and Master Son, Michael, the universe father and sovereign. Co-ordinate in divinity and complemental in creative attributes is the local universe Mother Spirit, the Divine Minister of Salvington. And these creators are in a very literal sense the Father-Son and the Spirit-Mother of all the native creatures of Nebadon." P37,PP1,PG406

> "Nevertheless, in dealing with sex creatures it is our custom to speak of those

beings of more direct descent from the Father and the Son as the Sons of God, while referring to the children of the Spirit as the daughters of God. Angels are, therefore, commonly designated by feminine pronouns on the sex planets." P38,S2,PP2,PG419

The following concepts may help in considering the validity of *The Urantia Book*:

- God is the Creator, and is good.

- Not only could God create intelligent life here on Earth, but elsewhere in the universe.

- Creation includes unseen (spiritual) friends such as angels and other types of sons and daughters of God that exist both here and elsewhere in the universe, and who can travel.

- Humans are capable of being contacted and being of service to God, depending upon their own will, their reliability, and God's will.

With these concepts, one can then imagine that, with appropriate authorization, a revelatory committee from the universes could be gathered together, and facts about the universe, its creation, its inhabitants, and about God could be imparted in written form to our planet, initially through a contact human, with the help of other humans, which is what happened.

CHAPTER 2: *THE URANTIA BOOK* - WHAT IS IT? WHO WROTE IT?

The Urantia Book reveals religious and factual truth. It is divided into four parts, each comprised of many individual chapters, which are called papers. Altogether, there are 196 papers.

The Urantia Book presents a wealth of information about the Creator and creation. This includes the creation of humans, nature, the universe, the inhabitants of the universe, and the characteristics and roles of the many types and orders of individuals in it. It portrays, in depth, the role of God, the creator, sustainer, and upholder. It portrays the structure and administration of the universe, and the relationship of the created individual to the Creator.

Before *The Urantia Book* was written, a request for it was made, which I discuss briefly in Chapter 10. Authorization to present the revelation to our planet, Urantia, was obtained from appropriate universe administrators, including superuniverse administrators 'on high.' Then, *The Urantia Book* was written by revelatory corps or commissions assembled for the purpose. The revelatory corps or commissions were comprised of a variety of types and orders of individual beings from throughout the universe of universes.

My understanding is that initial revelatory material was presented through a contact human, and that this initial material gathered the interest, belief, and participation of a larger human group. Subsequently, much of the book was materially manifested in written form. This process began in about 1910, and *The Urantia Book* was first published in 1955. The identity of the contact person is unknown and unimportant. These historic events continue to attract speculation and interest.

The Urantia Book dispels much mis-information, and this is helpful to truth seekers.

The Urantia Book has a Foreword that defines the terms it uses to describe various attributes of God and Creation. Since it is a revelation, some of the attributes, concepts, and distinctions are unfamiliar to us, which can make the Foreword seem difficult. For example, certain attributes of God and creation transcend time and space.

The first part of *The Urantia Book* is titled "The Central and Superuniverses." This part portrays the nature and attributes of God, the nature and magnitude of creation (the universe of universes), and God's relationship to creation. It reveals God's ministering personalities, along with many other types of central and superuniverse personalities/beings that exist, and their various orders and functions. God is very good, and the universe of universes is positive, and huge. An introduction to cosmic structure is presented in the next chapter.

> "The immensity of the far-flung creation of the Universal Father is utterly beyond the grasp of finite imagination; the enormousness of the master universe staggers the concept of even my order of being. But the mortal mind can be taught much about the plan and arrangement of the universes; you can know something of their physical

organization and marvelous administration; you may learn much about the various groups of intelligent beings who inhabit the seven superuniverses of time and the central universe of eternity." P12,PP1,PG128

One of the tenants of *The Urantia Book* is that we are not alone. There is life, organization, and beneficial administration in God's creation, beyond what we know here on Earth:

> "Your planet is a member of an enormous cosmos; you belong to a well-nigh infinite family of worlds, but your sphere is just as precisely administered and just as lovingly fostered as if it were the only inhabited world in all existence." P15,S14,PP9,PG183

The second part of *The Urantia Book* is titled "The Local Universe". It addresses the creation, composition, and administration of our local universe. It also portrays the many types of individual inhabitants who are created and live in our local universe, and their functions and relationships. Each local universe contains about ten million inhabited planets.

The third part of the book is titled "The History of Urantia" and presents the origin and history of our planet, including social, racial, biologic, and geologic history. For example:

> "Mammalian life continued to evolve. Enormous herds of horses joined the camels on the western plains of North America; this was truly the age of horses as well as of elephants. The horse's brain is next in animal quality to that of the elephant, but in one respect it is decidedly inferior, for the horse never fully overcame the deep-seated propensity to flee when frightened. The horse lacks the emotional control of the elephant, while the elephant is greatly handicapped by size and lack of agility. During this period an animal evolved which was somewhat like both the elephant and the horse, but it was soon destroyed by the rapidly increasing cat family." P61,S3,PP10,PG697

The fourth and last part, "The Life and Teachings of Jesus" re-presents, factually and in modern-day language, the life and teachings of Jesus. There are some differences between traditional Christianity and Urantia Book teachings, which I address briefly in Chapter 7, which is about Religion. God loves and dwells within all of us, and there are many wonderful people from all sorts of belief systems who know of God's love through their own personal experience.

Not only does *The Urantia Book* reveal factual information to us, it also challenges us. Some examples:

> "But the moment you lose sight of the spirit sovereignty of God the Father, some one religion will begin to assert its superiority over other religions; and then, instead of peace on earth and good will among men, there will start dissensions, recriminations, even religious wars, at least wars among religionists." P134,S4,PP8,PG1487

> "There is nothing incompatible between sonship in the spiritual kingdom and citizenship in the secular or civil government. It is the believer's duty to render to Caesar the things which are Caesar's and to God the things which are God's. There cannot be any disagreement between these two requirements, the one being material and the other spiritual, unless it should develop that a Caesar presumes to usurp the prerogatives of God and demand that spiritual homage and supreme worship be rendered to him. In such case you shall worship only God while you seek to enlighten such misguided earthly rulers and in this way lead them also to the recognition of the Father in heaven. You

shall not render spiritual worship to earthly rulers; neither should you employ the physical forces of earthly governments, whose rulers may sometime become believers, in the work of furthering the mission of the spiritual kingdom." P178,S1,PP3,PG1929 [Jesus teaching]

The Urantia Book is revealed religion. It is a bestowal or gift to this planet, a gift of information, of universal perspective, and of the Creator's perspective. However, *The Urantia Book* does not reveal everything.

"But no revelation short of the attainment of the Universal Father can ever be complete." P92,S4,PP9,PG1008

"Mankind should understand that we who participate in the revelation of truth are very rigorously limited by the instructions of our superiors. We are not at liberty to anticipate the scientific discoveries of a thousand years. Revelators must act in accordance with the instructions which form a part of the revelation mandate. We see no way of overcoming this difficulty, either now or at any future time. We full well know that, while the historic facts and religious truths of this series of revelatory presentations will stand on the records of the ages to come, within a few short years many of our statements regarding the physical sciences will stand in need of revision in consequence of additional scientific developments and new discoveries. These new developments we even now foresee, but we are forbidden to include such humanly undiscovered facts in the revelatory records. Let it be made clear that revelations are not necessarily inspired. The cosmology of these revelations is not inspired. It is limited by our permission for the co-ordination and sorting of present-day knowledge. While divine or spiritual insight is a gift, human wisdom must evolve." P101,S4,PP2,PG1109

"Revealed religion is the unifying element of human existence. Revelation unifies history, co-ordinates geology, astronomy, physics, chemistry, biology, sociology, and psychology. Spiritual experience is the real soul of man's cosmos." P102,S4,PP6,PG1123

Chapter 2

CHAPTER 3: CREATOR, CREATION, AND COSMOLOGY

God is very good. *The Urantia Book* consistently describes God's attributes in terms such as "...infinite goodness, endless mercy, matchless wisdom, and superb character." P1,S4,PP4,PG26 As another example: "God is inherently kind, naturally compassionate, and everlastingly merciful." P2,S4,PP2,PG38

God is love, goodness, spirit, personality, and so much more. As well as personal attributes, there are also impersonal and undeified aspects of God which are also positive realities. There are aspects of God that transcend time and space. There is an evolutionary aspect of God, to which we as co-creators can add to, and in which material, spiritual, and in-between realities are coordinated. There are feminine attributes of God, which I discuss more in Chapters 1 and 6, and God is mystery: "The infinity of the perfection of God is such that it eternally constitutes his mystery." P1,S4,PP1,PG26

The Eternal Paradise Trinity consists of the Universal Father, the Eternal Son, and the Infinite Spirit. God is self-distributive. However, there is complete Deity unity. The Paradise Trinity and all other attributes of God are divinely One. Divinity is the co-ordinating and unifying element of all aspects of God. There is only one First Cause, or First Source and Center.

> "The Universal Father is the God of all creation, the First Source and Center of all things and beings. First think of God as a creator, then as a controller, and lastly as an infinite upholder. ..." P1,PP1,PG21

> "... The Trinity is Deity unity, and this unity rests eternally upon the absolute foundations of the divine oneness of the three original and co-ordinate and coexistent personalities, God the Father, God the Son, and God the Spirit." P10,PP2,PG108

Creation is immense. The master universe, or simply creation, has a gravity center, the central Isle of Paradise. The Isle of Paradise is the dwelling place of the Paradise Trinity. Around and including the central Isle of Paradise is Havona, a perfect, eternal, divine, harmonious, and beautiful central universe.

> "The perfect and divine universe [Havona] occupies the center of all creation; it is the central core around which the vast creations of time and space revolve. Paradise is the gigantic nuclear Isle of absolute stability which rests motionless at the very heart of the magnificent eternal universe. ... It is of enormous dimensions and almost unbelievable mass and consists of one billion spheres of unimagined beauty and superb grandeur..." P14,PP1,PG152

> "... But the depths of the spiritual beauty and the wonders of this magnificent

ensemble [The Isle of Paradise] are utterly beyond the comprehension of the finite mind of material creatures. ..." P11,PP2,PG118

Elliptically orbiting around Havona are seven huge, evolutionary, superuniverses. The central Isle of Paradise, the central universe Havona, and the seven superuniverses are all inhabited. Together, they are called the grand universe.

> "The myriads of planetary systems were all made to be eventually inhabited by many different types of intelligent creatures, beings who could know God, receive the divine affection, and love him in return. The universe of universes is the work of God and the dwelling place of his diverse creatures. "God created the heavens and formed the earth; he established the universe and created this world not in vain; he formed it to be inhabited.""" P1,PP2,PG21

Outside the seven superuniverses, vast regions of space exhibit "... stupendous circuits of force and materializing energies ..." P12,S1,PP8,PG130. There are four of these outer space levels.

> "We know very little of the significance of these tremendous phenomena of outer space. A greater creation of the future is in process of formation. We can observe its immensity, we can discern its extent and sense its majestic dimensions, but otherwise we know little more about these realms than do the astronomers of Urantia. As far as we know, no material beings on the order of humans, no angels or other spirit creatures, exist in this outer ring of nebulae, suns, and planets. This distant domain is beyond the jurisdiction and administration of the superuniverse governments." P12,S2,PP5,PG131

There are approximately seven trillion inhabited planets altogether. Each of the seven evolutionary superuniverses includes about one trillion inhabited worlds.

For administration, each 1,000 inhabited planets comprises a system, and 100 systems comprise a constellation. One hundred constellations comprise a local universe, 100 local universes comprise a minor sector, 100 minor sectors comprise a major sector, and 10 major sectors comprise one of the seven superuniverses.

These concepts are displayed on the following pages. A diagram of our local system is presented in Chapter 11.

Our local system, Satania, has "... 619 inhabited worlds ... located in over five hundred different physical systems. Only five [of these physical systems] have more than two inhabited worlds, and of these only one has four peopled planets, while there are forty-six having two inhabited worlds." P32,S2,PP10,PG359 [I interpret 'physical systems' in this context to mean solar systems.]

There are three classifications of inhabitants in the universes: Descending Sons of God, Ascending Sons of God, and Trinitized Sons of God (and I'm sure these classifications include Daughters of God also). I will focus on the ascenders and descenders.

> "Descending orders of sonship include personalities who are of direct and divine creation. Ascending sons, such as mortal creatures, achieve this status by experiential participation in the creative technique known as evolution. ..." P20,PP2,PG223

> "All descending Sons of God have high and divine origins. They are dedicated to the descending ministry of service on the worlds and systems of time and space, there to

- OUR LOCAL UNIVERSE, NEBADON
  Contains ten million inhabited planets.

- OUR MAJOR SECTOR, SPLANDON
  Contains 100 billion inhabited planets.

- OUR SUPERUNIVERSE, ORVONTON
  Contains one trillion inhabited planets. The Milky Way is the main plane of Orvonton. Orvonton contains most stars visible to us, and as of about 1935, our astronomers had recognized 8 of its 10 major sectors.

- ISLE OF PARADISE
  - Is the "... most gigantic organized body of cosmic reality in all the Master Universe..." 11:0
  - Is the gravity center of the universe of universes.
  - Is eternal, stationary, non-spatial, and non-temporal (transcends space and time).
  - Is made of Paradise, and is both a material creation and a spiritual abode.
  - "Paradise is the center of all creation, the source of all energies, and the place of primal origin of all personalities." 11:9
  - It "... exists primarily as the dwelling place of Deity ...". It is the home of the Creator, and the Paradise Trinity, who are divinely one. 11:1
  - "But the depths of spiritual beauty and the wonders of this magnificent ensemble are utterly beyond the comprehension of the finite mind of material creatures." 11:0

- 21 SATELLITE SPHERES
  - Enormous, sacred, eternal, rotate clockwise.
  - Innermost circuit: the seven "... secret spheres of the Universal Father ..." 13:0
  - Middle circuit: the seven "... luminous worlds of the Eternal Son ..." 13:0
  - Outermost circuit: the seven "... immense spheres of the Infinite Spirit ...", which are the "... executive-headquarters worlds of the Seven Master Spirits..." (one for each superuniverse). 13:0

- HAVONA, THE CENTRAL UNIVERSE
  - Contains one billion inhabited spheres of "... unimagined beauty and superb grandeur ..." 14:0
  - Perfect, harmonious, eternal, and enormous.
  - In seven concentric circuits orbiting clockwise.
  - Architecturally created, not evolutionary.

- DARK GRAVITY BODIES
  - Two counter-rotating belts containing "... an unbelievable number ..." of dark gravity bodies which hide Havona "... from the view of even near-by inhabited universes of time and space." 14:1
  - Of "...extraordinary mass...", the inner belt rotates counterclockwise, the outer clockwise. They act as universe stabilizers. 14:1

THE GRAND UNIVERSE
(INHABITED)

MAP VIEW

A limited conceptual interpretation based on The Urantia Book revelation. All quotes are from The Urantia Book
11:9 refers to Paper 11, Section 9
Not to Scale

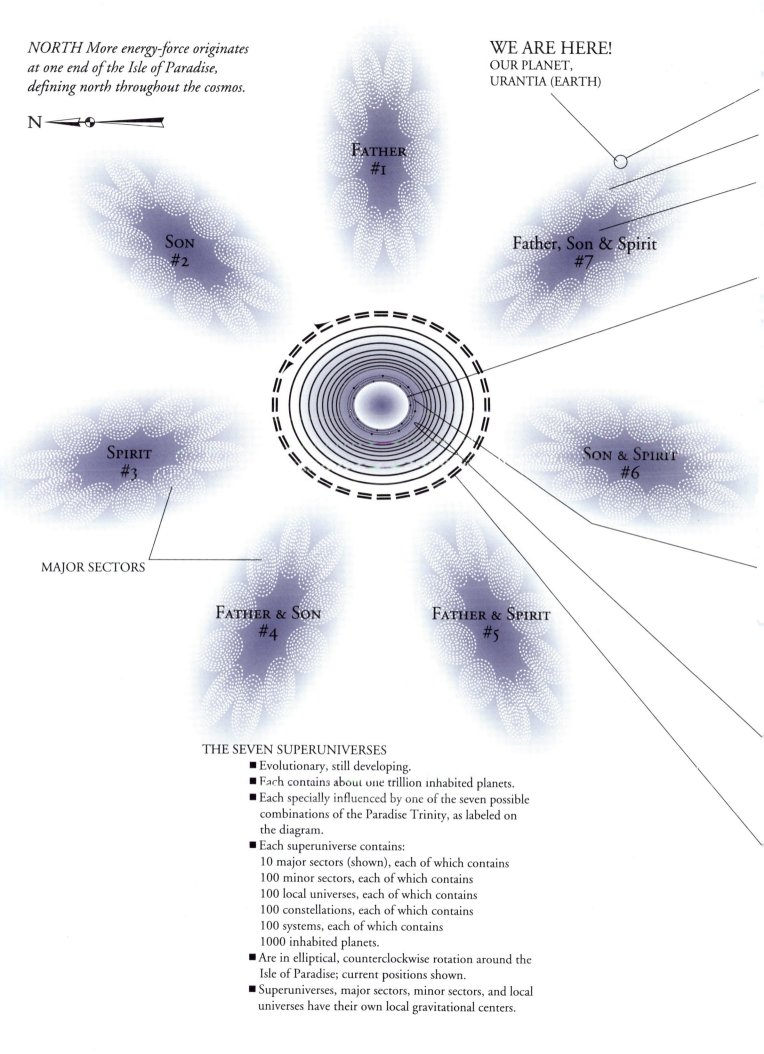

> facilitate the progress in the Paradise climb of the lowly creatures of evolutionary origin—the ascending sons of God. ..." P20,S1,PP1,PG223

Ascenders grow, learn, and progress through personal choice and experience upward and inward toward God. Humans are ascending daughters and sons of God. We are created by the evolutionary technique here on the planetary level.

> "... Urantians benefit by the spiritual influences and activities of the local and the superuniverse, with their almost endless array of loving personalities who ever lead the true of purpose and the honest of heart upward and inward towards the ideals of divinity and the goal of supreme perfection." P9,S2,PP4,PG100

The descending daughters/sons are directly created, and there are many types and functions throughout the universe of universes. Most are non-material (spiritual) beings. For example, Melchizedek Sons, Vorondadek Sons, Lanonandek Sons, and Life Carrier Sons are descending Sons of local universe origin, while Creator Sons are of Paradise origin.

There are two types of material spheres in the universe, evolutionary and architecturalized. Architecturalized spheres are directly created, whereas the solar and planetary systems we are familiar with are created by the technique of evolution. The headquarters spheres of our local universe, and the billion perfect spheres comprising the perfect central universe of Havona, are architecturalized.

Creation of suns and planets, which are evolutionary systems, goes something like this:

The Paradise Trinity consists of the Universal Father, the Eternal Son, and the Infinite Spirit. When the Father and Son participate in a certain type of creative interaction, they give birth to a Creator Son. Creator Sons are schooled in the central universe, and then, in association with a daughter of the Infinite Spirit, position themselves in space. Then, from space potential, and with the help of other orders of beings, they mobilize, create, and materialize the whirling gasses, etc., from which evolutionary solar and planetary systems emerge. In this way, a Creator Son, working with a Daughter of the Infinite Spirit, creates a local universe of solar and planetary systems. These created systems are not harmonized and perfect, they are evolutionary. For example, meteors can and do collide with planets.

> "When the fullness of absolute spiritual ideation in the Eternal Son encounters the fullness of absolute personality concept in the Universal Father, ... then, right then and there, ... there flashes into full-fledged being a new and original Creator Son, the only-begotten Son of the perfect ideal and the powerful idea whose union produces this new creator personality of power and perfection." P21,S1,PP1,PG234

> "When energy-matter has attained a certain stage in mass materialization, a Paradise Creator Son appears upon the scene, accompanied by a Creative Daughter of the Infinite Spirit. Simultaneously with the arrival of the Creator Son, work is begun upon the architectural sphere which is to become the headquarters world of the projected local universe. For long ages such a local creation evolves, suns become stabilized, planets form and swing into their orbits, while the work of creating the architectural worlds which are to serve as constellation headquarters and system capitals continues." P32,S1,PP5,PG358

Once an evolutionary planet is stable enough to support life, life plasma is usually carried from life laboratories of the local universe headquarters spheres and placed on the planet. This task is performed by Life Carriers, an order of local universe sons of God, and who carry life to, and foster it on, the planets. On Urantia (Earth) it was a little different:

> "That we are called Life Carriers should not confuse you. We can and do carry life to the planets, but we brought no life to Urantia. Urantia life is unique, original with the planet. This sphere is a life-modification world; all life appearing hereon was formulated by us right here on the planet; and there is no other world in all Satania, even in all Nebadon, that has a life existence just like that of Urantia. [Satania is the name of our local system, and Nebadon is the name of our local universe.]
>
> *550,000,000* years ago the Life Carrier corps returned to Urantia. In co-operation with spiritual powers and superphysical forces we organized and initiated the original life patterns of this world and planted them in the hospitable waters of the realm. All planetary life (aside from extraplanetary personalities) ..., had its origin in our three original, identical, and simultaneous marine-life implantations. These three life implantations have been designated as: the *central* or Eurasian-African, the *eastern* or Australasian, and the *western*, embracing Greenland and the Americas." P58,S4,PP1,PG667

The implanted life plasma is 'programmed' in accordance with divine plans. Part of this programming is that only one 'will creature' or human is created on any one planet.

On our planet, the life plasma evolved into the plant and animal kingdoms, and evolution on our planet has occurred much as our scientists have deduced. However, our scientists have not deduced the role of God in creation. They have not concluded that our life plasma was formulated here by Life Carriers. And, until maybe recently, our scientists have not deduced that evolution can sometimes proceed by leaps or steps, rather than always being slow and steady:

> "... you will not be able to find such connecting links between the great divisions of the animal kingdom nor between the highest of the prehuman animal types and the dawn men of the human races. These so-called "missing links" will forever remain missing, for the simple reason that they never existed.
>
> From era to era radically new species of animal life arise. They do not evolve as the result of the gradual accumulation of small variations; they appear as full-fledged and new orders of life, and they appear *suddenly*.
>
> The *sudden* appearance of new species and diversified orders of living organisms is wholly biologic, strictly natural. There is nothing supernatural connected with these genetic mutations." P58,S6,PP2,PG669

On Urantia, the first two humans were a brother and sister, who were an evolutionary jump ahead of the primates who had parented them.

> "From the year A.D. 1934 back to the birth of the first two human beings is just 993,419 years." P62,S5,PP1,PG707

> "These first two humans—the twins—were a great trial to their Primates parents. They were so curious and adventurous that they nearly lost their lives on numerous occasions before they were eight years old. As it was, they were rather well scarred up by the time they were twelve.

Very early they learned to engage in verbal communication; by the age of ten they had worked out an improved sign and word language of almost half a hundred ideas and had greatly improved and expanded the crude communicative technique of their ancestors. But try as hard as they might, they were able to teach only a few of their new signs and symbols to their parents.

When about nine years of age, they journeyed off down the river one bright day and held a momentous conference. Every celestial intelligence stationed on Urantia, including myself, was present as an observer of the transactions of this noontide tryst. On this eventful day they arrived at an understanding to live with and for each other, and this was the first of a series of such agreements which finally culminated in the decision to flee from their inferior animal associates and to journey northward, little knowing that they were thus to found the human race." P62,S5,PP6,PG708

It is interesting to me that the religionists on our planet, and the scientists, are both right, partly, in the controversy about creationism versus evolution.

Chapter 3

CHAPTER 4: PLANETARY HISTORY AND DISPENSATIONS

a. *Introduction*

The third section of *The Urantia Book*, "The History of Urantia," begins with papers with titles such as "The Origin of Urantia," "Life Establishment on Urantia," "The Marine-Life Era on Urantia." In these and others, the physical and biological history of our planet is presented and discussed.

For example:

> "The northern regions of this world have experienced six separate and distinct ice invasions, although there were scores of advances and recessions associated with the activity of each individual ice sheet. The ice in North America collected in two and, later, three centers. Greenland was covered, and Iceland was completely buried beneath the ice flow. In Europe the ice at various times covered the British Isles excepting the coast of southern England, and it overspread western Europe down to France." P61,S5,PP4,PG699

> "*750,000,000* years ago the first breaks in the continental land mass began as the great north-and-south cracking, which later admitted the ocean waters and prepared the way for the westward drift of the continents of North and South America, including Greenland. The long east-and-west cleavage separated Africa from Europe and severed the land masses of Australia, the Pacific Islands, and Antarctica from the Asiatic continent." P57,S8,PP23,PG663 [Not bad for a book published before continental drift was generally accepted.]

And concerning dinosaurs:

> "These massive creatures became less active and strong as they grew larger and larger; but they required such an enormous amount of food and the land was so overrun by them that they literally starved to death and became extinct—they lacked the intelligence to cope with the situation." P60,S2,PP3,PG687

Social, racial, and religious history are also presented, as indicated by paper titles such as "The Evolutionary Races of Color," "The Dawn of Civilization," "The Evolution of Human Government," "Andite Expansion in the Orient," "Development of Modern Civilization," "The Evolution of Marriage," "Fetishes, Charms, and Magic," "The Evolution of Prayer," "Social Problems in Religion", etc.

For example:

> "On an average evolutionary planet the six evolutionary races of color appear one by one; the red man is the first to evolve, and for ages he roams the world before

the succeeding colored races make their appearance. The simultaneous emergence of all six races on Urantia, *and in one family,* was most unusual." P64,S6,PP1,PG722 [The six colors are red, blue, orange, yellow, green, and indigo.]

"Primitive men are mighty hunters and fierce fighters. The law of this age is the physical survival of the fittest; the government of these times is wholly tribal. During the early racial struggles on many worlds some of the evolutionary races are obliterated, as occurred on Urantia." P52,S1,PP3,PG589 [The orange and green men were essentially obliterated, and the blue races blended.]

"About eighty-five thousand years ago the comparatively pure remnants of the red race went en masse across to North America, and shortly thereafter the Bering land isthmus sank, thus isolating them. No red man ever returned to Asia. But throughout Siberia, China, central Asia, India, and Europe they left behind much of their stock blended with the other colored races." P64,S6,PP5,PG723

"Woman was long denied full freedom of self-disposal in marriage, but the more intelligent women have always been able to circumvent this restriction by the clever exercise of their wits. Man has usually taken the lead in courtship, but not always. Woman sometimes formally, as well as covertly, initiates marriage. And as civilization has progressed, women have had an increasing part in all phases of courtship and marriage." P83,S2,PP4,PG923

"These early Neanderthalers could hardly be called sun worshipers. They rather lived in fear of the dark; they had a mortal dread of nightfall. As long as the moon shone a little, they managed to get along, but in the dark of the moon they grew panicky and began the sacrifice of their best specimens of manhood and womanhood in an effort to induce the moon again to shine." P64,S4,PP13,PG722

Human society evolves from the first primitives, all the way to being "settled in light and life" (we still have a way to go). It is the Creator's will that any race of humans, once started, evolves all the way until settled in light and life.

Along this evolutionary journey to light and life, there are various planetary administrative epochs or dispensations, and this is true for all inhabited planets. These epochs or dispensations are related to revelatory bestowals (gifts) that planets receive from time to time in the course of their evolution. The purpose of the revelatory bestowals, which are revelations of truth, is to foster progress toward light and life.

"The religious tendencies of the human races are innate; they are universally manifested and have an apparently natural origin; primitive religions are always evolutionary in their genesis. As natural religious experience continues to progress, periodic revelations of truth punctuate the otherwise slow-moving course of planetary evolution." P103,PP2,PG1129

The remainder of this chapter presents a summary of the epochs or dispensations that a typical inhabited planet experiences on its way to becoming settled in light and life, along with a summary of the epochs as they have occurred so far here on Urantia, which are unusual. For example, our first planetary spiritual administrator joined a rebellion against God. (This rebellion is discussed more fully in the next chapter.)

Planetary History and Dispensations — Chapter 4

Each planetary epoch typically lasts for tens to hundreds of thousands of years.

> "From the inception of life on an evolutionary planet to the time of its final flowering in the era of light and life, there appear upon the stage of world action at least seven epochs of human life. These successive ages are determined by the planetary missions of the divine Sons, and on an average inhabited world these epochs appear in the following order:
>
> 1. Pre-Planetary Prince Man.
> 2. Post-Planetary Prince Man.
> 3. Post-Adamic Man.
> 4. Post-Magisterial Son Man.
> 5. Post-Bestowal Son Man.
> 6. Post-Teacher Son Man.
> 7. The Era of Light and Life." P52,PP1,PG589

b. *The Planetary Prince*

This is a spiritual being, a local universe descending son of God, who is assigned as an administrator of the planet. Our Planetary Prince, Caligastia, "was a Lanonandek Son, number 9,344 of the secondary order." P66,S1,PP1,PG741

> "From the time of man's emergence from the animal level—when he can choose to worship the Creator—to the arrival of the Planetary Prince, mortal will creatures are called *primitive men*. There are six basic types or races of primitive men, and these early peoples successively appear in the order of the spectrum colors, beginning with the red. The length of time consumed in this early life evolution varies greatly on the different worlds, ranging from one hundred and fifty thousand years to over one million years of Urantia time.
>
> The evolutionary races of color—red, orange, yellow, green, blue, and indigo—begin to appear about the time that primitive man is developing a simple language and is beginning to exercise the creative imagination. By this time man is well accustomed to standing erect." P52,S1,PP1,PG589

> "Within one hundred thousand years from the time man acquires erect posture, the Planetary Prince usually arrives, having been dispatched by the System Sovereign upon report of the Life Carriers that will is functioning, even though comparatively few individuals have thus developed. Primitive mortals usually welcome the Planetary Prince and his visible staff; in fact they often look upon them with awe and reverence, almost with worshipfulness, if they are not restrained." P52,S1,PP8,PG590

> "With the arrival of the Planetary Prince a new dispensation begins. Government appears on earth, and the advanced tribal epoch is attained. Great social strides are made during a few thousand years of this regime. Under normal conditions mortals attain a high state of civilization during this age. They do not struggle so long in barbarism as did the Urantia races. But life on an inhabited world is so changed by rebellion that you can have little or no idea of such a regime on a normal planet." P52,S2,PP1,PG591

> "When the Planetary Prince arrives on a primitive world, the evolved religion of fear and ignorance prevails. The prince and his staff make the first revelations of higher

truth and universe organization. These initial presentations of revealed religion are very simple, and they usually pertain to the affairs of the local system. Religion is wholly an evolutionary process prior to the arrival of the Planetary Prince. Subsequently, religion progresses by graduated revelation as well as by evolutionary growth. Each dispensation, each mortal epoch, receives an enlarged presentation of spiritual truth and religious ethics. The evolution of the religious capacity of receptivity in the inhabitants of a world largely determines their rate of spiritual advancement and the extent of religious revelation." P52,S2,PP3,PG591

"On going to a young world, a Planetary Prince usually takes with him a group of volunteer ascending beings from the local system headquarters. These ascenders accompany the prince as advisers and helpers in the work of early race improvement. This corps of material helpers constitutes the connecting link between the prince and the world races. The Urantia Prince, Caligastia, had a corps of one hundred such helpers." P50,S3,PP1,PG574

"The Life Carriers, the architects of form, provide such volunteers with new physical bodies, which they occupy for the periods of their planetary sojourn." P50,S3,PP3,PG574

The Planetary prince's material helpers, the corporeal staff, has special characteristics; they differ from the evolutionary humans. The creation of midwayers on a planet, and references to mighty men of old, who had exceptional longevity, result from special attributes of the corporeal staff. Midwayers are planetary inhabitants who exist midway between mortals, who are material, and angels, who are spiritual.

On our planet, the corporeal staff, the Caligastia one hundred, were specially constructed humans, you might say. One hundred ascending citizens on Jerusem, our system headquarters, were selected from volunteers, were brought here by seraphic transport, and were given specially constructed human bodies containing life plasma contributed by 100 mortal humans (fifty men and fifty women). This specially constructed corporeal staff were attuned to the life circuits of the system and were immortal, as long as they had the fruit from a literal "tree of life", which was a shrub brought from Edentia, our constellation headquarters. The "tree of life" was of no use to evolutionary humans. The Caligastia 100 were created for planetary service. Up until the rebellion, they were teachers to the native humans. The one hundred evolutionary humans who donated their life plasma were also encircuited with the life circuits of the system, were also immortal, and were the personal assistants to the Calagastia 100.

"These transactions, together with the literal creation of special bodies for the Caligastia one hundred, gave origin to numerous legends, many of which subsequently became confused with the later traditions concerning the planetary installation of Adam and Eve". P66,S2,PP8,PG742

"The arrival of the Prince's staff created a profound impression. While it required almost a thousand years for the news to spread abroad, those tribes near the Mesopotamian headquarters were tremendously influenced by the teachings and conduct of the one hundred new sojourners on Urantia. And much of your subsequent mythology grew out of the garbled legends of these early days when these members of the Prince's staff were repersonalized on Urantia as supermen." P66,S4,PP1,PG743

> "The postrebellion era on Urantia witnessed many unusual happenings. A great civilization—the culture of Dalamatia—was going to pieces. "The Nephilim (Nodites) were on earth in those days, and when these sons of the gods went in to the daughters of men and they bore to them, their children were the 'mighty men of old,' the 'men of renown.'" While hardly "sons of the gods," the staff and their early descendants were so regarded by the evolutionary mortals of those distant days; even their stature came to be magnified by tradition. This, then, is the origin of the well-nigh universal folk tale of the gods who came down to earth and there with the daughters of men begot an ancient race of heroes." P77,S2,PP3,PG856

> "The prince's corporeal staff early organize the planetary schools of training and culture, wherein the cream of the evolutionary races are instructed and then sent forth to teach these better ways to their people. These schools of the prince are located at the material headquarters of the planet." P50,S4,PP1,PG575

> "A Planetary Prince is not visible to mortal beings; it is a test of faith to believe the representations of the semimaterial beings of his staff. But these schools of culture and training are well adapted to the needs of each planet, and there soon develops a keen and laudatory rivalry among the races of men in their efforts to gain entrance to these various institutions of learning." P50,S4,PP9,PG575

When the Caligastia one hundred, 50 males and 50 females, had a type of liaison, they created the primary midwayers. Fifty thousand primary midwayers were thus created, who were helpful in accomplishing the Planetary Prince's work.

> "On Urantia these plans for planetary progress and cultural advancement were well under way, proceeding most satisfactorily, when the whole enterprise was brought to a rather sudden and most inglorious end by Caligastia's adherence to the Lucifer rebellion. [Caligastia was our Planetary Prince. The rebellion is subsequently discussed.]
> It was one of the most profoundly shocking episodes of this rebellion for me to learn of the callous perfidy of one of my own order of sonship, Caligastia, who, in deliberation and with malice aforethought, systematically perverted the instruction and poisoned the teaching provided in all the Urantia planetary schools in operation at that time. The wreck of these schools was speedy and complete." P50,S4,PP11,PG576

c. *The Material Son and Daughter*

> "When the original impetus of evolutionary life has run its biologic course, when man has reached the apex of animal development, there arrives the second order of sonship, and the second dispensation of grace and ministry is inaugurated. This is true on all evolutionary worlds. When the highest possible level of evolutionary life has been attained, when primitive man has ascended as far as possible in the biologic scale, a Material Son and Daughter always appear on the planet, having been dispatched by the System Sovereign." P52,S3,PP1,PG592 [The System Sovereign is a local universe son of God who is the administrator of our local system, Satania.]

> "A Planetary Adam and Eve are, in potential, the full gift of physical grace to the mortal races. The chief business of such an imported pair is to multiply and to uplift the children of time. But there is no immediate interbreeding between the people of the

garden and those of the world; for many generations Adam and Eve remain biologically segregated from the evolutionary mortals while they build up a strong race of their order. This is the origin of the violet race on the inhabited worlds." P51,S3,PP3,PG583

"It is the prime purpose of the Adamic regime to influence evolving man to complete the transit from the hunter and herder stage of civilization to that of the agriculturist and horticulturist, to be later supplemented by the appearance of the urban and industrial adjuncts to civilization. Ten thousand years of this dispensation of the biologic uplifters is sufficient to effect a marvelous transformation. Twenty-five thousand years of such an administration of the conjoint wisdom of the Planetary Prince and the Material Sons usually ripens the sphere for the advent of a Magisterial Son." P52,S3,PP3,PG593

"The post-Adamic epoch is the dispensation of internationalism. With the near completion of the task of race blending, nationalism wanes, and the brotherhood of man really begins to materialize. Representative government begins to take the place of the monarchial or paternal form of rulership. The educational system becomes world-wide, and gradually the languages of the races give way to the tongue of the violet people. Universal peace and co-operation are seldom attained until the races are fairly well blended, and until they speak a common language." P52,S3,PP10,PG594

"Great ethical advancement characterizes this era; the brotherhood of man is the goal of its society. World-wide peace—the cessation of race conflict and national animosity—is the indicator of planetary ripeness for the advent of the third order of sonship, the Magisterial Son." P52,S3,PP12,PG594

About 38,000 years ago our Material Son and Daughter, Adam and Eve, came to our rebellion-scarred planet, defaulted, and only accomplished part of their planetary mission as biologic uplifters. I discuss their default in the next chapter. They are sex creatures, and are biologically superior to humans. On a normal planet, they, along with the Planetary Prince, would still be here, working for planetary betterment. Upon their default, they lost their planetary immortality, and their offspring were given the choice to stay or return to system headquarters. Some stayed, interbred with, and improved the evolutionary races of humans, and some returned.

"Adams and Eves are semimaterial creatures and, as such, are not transportable by seraphim. They must undergo dematerialization on the system capital before they can be enseraphimed for transport to the world of assignment. The transport seraphim are able to effect such changes in the Material Sons and in other semimaterial beings as enable them to be enseraphimed and thus to be transported through space from one world or system to another. About three days of standard time are consumed in this transport preparation, and it requires the co-operation of a Life Carrier to restore such a dematerialized creature to normal existence upon arrival at the end of the seraphic-transport journey." P51,S2,PP2,PG582

"The Planetary Adam and Eve of Urantia were members of the senior corps of Material Sons on Jerusem, being jointly number 14,311. They belonged to the third physical series and were a little more than eight feet in height." P74,S1,PP2,PG828

"The bodies of Adam and Eve gave forth a shimmer of light, but they always wore clothing in conformity with the custom of their associates. Though wearing very little during the day, at eventide they donned night wraps. The origin of the traditional halo encircling the heads of supposed pious and holy men dates back to the days of Adam and Eve. Since the light emanations of their bodies were so largely obscured by clothing, only the radiating glow from their heads was discernible. The descendants of Adamson always thus portrayed their concept of individuals believed to be extraordinary in spiritual development.

Adam and Eve could communicate with each other and with their immediate children over a distance of about fifty miles. This thought exchange was effected by means of the delicate gas chambers located in close proximity to their brain structures. By this mechanism they could send and receive thought oscillations. But this power was instantly suspended upon the mind's surrender to the discord and disruption of evil." P74,S6,PP5,PG834

"Eve did not suffer pain in childbirth; neither did the early evolutionary races. Only the mixed races produced by the union of evolutionary man with the Nodites and later with the Adamites suffered the severe pangs of childbirth.

Adam and Eve, like their brethren on Jerusem, were energized by dual nutrition, subsisting on both food and light, supplemented by certain superphysical energies unrevealed on Urantia. Their Urantia offspring did not inherit the parental endowment of energy intake and light circulation. They had a single circulation, the human type of blood sustenance. They were designedly mortal though long-lived, albeit longevity gravitated toward the human norm with each succeeding generation." P76,S4,PP2,PG850

"The body cells of the Material Sons and their progeny are far more resistant to disease than are those of the evolutionary beings indigenous to the planet. The body cells of the native races are akin to the living disease-producing microscopic and ultramicroscopic organisms of the realm. These facts explain why the Urantia peoples must do so much by way of scientific effort to withstand so many physical disorders. You would be far more disease resistant if your races carried more of the Adamic life." P76,S4,PP7,PG851

"The "golden age" is a myth, but Eden was a fact, and the Garden civilization was actually overthrown. Adam and Eve carried on in the Garden for one hundred and seventeen years when, through the impatience of Eve and the errors of judgment of Adam, they presumed to turn aside from the ordained way, speedily bringing disaster upon themselves and ruinous retardation upon the developmental progression of all Urantia." P74,S8,PP14,PG838

"The human race has been uplifted despite the immediate consequences of the Adamic default. Although the divine plan of giving the violet race to the Urantia peoples miscarried, the mortal races have profited enormously from the limited contribution which Adam and his descendants made to the Urantia races." P75,S8,PP1,PG845

d. *The Magisterial Son*

Urantia has not yet had a Magisterial Son.

"On normal and loyal planets this age opens with the mortal races blended and biologically fit. There are no race or color problems; literally all nations and races are of one blood. The brotherhood of man flourishes, and the nations are learning to live on earth in peace and tranquillity. Such a world stands on the eve of a great and culminating intellectual development.

When an evolutionary world becomes thus ripe for the magisterial age, one of the high order of Avonal Sons makes his appearance on a magisterial mission. The Planetary Prince and the Material Sons are of local universe origin; the Magisterial Son hails from Paradise." P52,S4,PP1,PG594

"Each new dispensation extends the horizon of revealed religion, and the Magisterial Sons extend the revelation of truth to portray the affairs of the local universe and all its tributaries.

After the initial visitation of a Magisterial Son the races soon effect their economic liberation. The daily work required to sustain one's independence would be represented by two and one-half hours of your time. It is perfectly safe to liberate such ethical and intelligent mortals. Such refined peoples well know how to utilize leisure for self-improvement and planetary advancement. This age witnesses the further purification of the racial stocks by the restriction of reproduction among the less fit and poorly endowed individuals." P52,S4,PP4,PG594

e. *The Bestowal Son*

The quotes in this section may be aided by the following: local universe Creator Sons are of the order of Michaels. Our local universe is named Nebadon, so our local universe Creator Son is Michael of Nebadon.

We have had a Bestowal Son here on earth, Jesus Christ. As we shall see, our Bestowal Son was our local universe Creator Son, Michael of Nebadon. So our bestowal Son, Jesus Christ, Michael of Nebadon, and Christ Michael are all one and the same.

"Some order of Paradise Son must be bestowed upon each mortal-inhabited world in order to make it possible for Thought Adjusters to indwell the minds of all normal human beings on that sphere, for the Adjusters do not come to all bona fide human beings until the Spirit of Truth has been poured out upon all flesh; and the sending of the Spirit of Truth is dependent upon the return to universe headquarters of a Paradise Son who has successfully executed a mission of mortal bestowal upon an evolving world." P20,S5,PP3,PG227 [Thought Adjusters are the fragments of the Heavenly Father that indwell the human mind.]

"On a mortal-bestowal mission a Paradise Son is always born of woman and grows up as a male child of the realm, as Jesus did on Urantia. These Sons of supreme service all pass from infancy through youth to manhood just as does a human being. In every respect they become like the mortals of the race into which they are born. They make petitions to the Father as do the children of the realms in which they serve. From a material viewpoint, these human-divine Sons live ordinary lives with just one exception: They do not beget offspring on the worlds of their sojourn; that is a universal restriction imposed on all orders of the Paradise bestowal Sons." P20,S6,PP2,PG229

"When a certain standard of intellectual and spiritual development is attained on an inhabited world, a Paradise bestowal Son always arrives. On normal worlds he does not appear in the flesh until the races have ascended to the highest levels of intellectual development and ethical attainment. But on Urantia the bestowal Son, even your own Creator Son, appeared at the close of the Adamic dispensation, but that is not the usual order of events on the worlds of space." P52,S5,PP1,PG595

"When the worlds have become ripe for spiritualization, the bestowal Son arrives. These Sons always belong to the Magisterial or Avonal order except in that case, once in each local universe, when the Creator Son prepares for his terminal bestowal on some evolutionary world, as occurred when Michael of Nebadon appeared on Urantia to bestow himself upon your mortal races. Only one world in near ten million can enjoy such a gift; all other worlds are spiritually advanced by the bestowal of a Paradise Son of the Avonal order." P52,S5,PP2,PG595 [Magisterial or Avonal Sons, and Creator Sons, are from Paradise.]

"The bestowal Son lives and dies for the spiritual uplift of the mortal races of a world. He establishes the "new and living way"; his life is an incarnation of Paradise truth in mortal flesh, that very truth—even the Spirit of Truth—in the knowledge of which men shall be free." P52,S5,PP4,PG596

"Upon the resurrection of a bestowal Son, on the third day after yielding up his incarnated life, he ascends to the right hand of the Universal Father, receives the assurance of the acceptance of the bestowal mission, and returns to the Creator Son at the headquarters of the local universe. Thereupon the bestowal Avonal and the Creator Michael send their joint spirit, the Spirit of Truth, into the bestowal world. This is the occasion when the "spirit of the triumphant Son is poured out upon all flesh." The Universe Mother Spirit also participates in this bestowal of the Spirit of Truth, and concomitant therewith there issues the bestowal edict of the Thought Adjusters. Thereafter all normal-minded will creatures of that world will receive Adjusters as soon as they attain the age of moral responsibility, of spiritual choice." P52,S5,PP6,PG596

"The bestowal Son is the Prince of Peace. He arrives with the message, "Peace on earth and good will among men." On normal worlds this is a dispensation of world-wide peace; the nations no more learn war. But such salutary influences did not attend the coming of your bestowal Son, Christ Michael. Urantia is not proceeding in the normal order. Your world is out of step in the planetary procession. Your Master, when on earth, warned his disciples that his advent would not bring the usual reign of peace on Urantia. He distinctly told them that there would be "wars and rumors of wars," and that nation would rise against nation. At another time he said, "Think not that I have come to bring peace upon earth." P52,S6,PP1,PG597

"If you could be transplanted from your backward and confused world to some normal planet now in the postbestowal Son age, you would think you had been translated to the heaven of your traditions. You would hardly believe that you were observing the normal evolutionary workings of a mortal sphere of human habitation. These worlds are in the spiritual circuits of their realm, and they enjoy all the advantages of the universe broadcasts and the reflectivity services of the superuniverse." P52,S6,PP8,PG598

[Our planet was cut off from universe communications during the rebellion, which is discussed in the next chapter. Reflectivity is a means of direct communication via angelic orders of beings; they reflect truth from one location in the universe to another.]

f. *The Trinity Teacher Sons*

Urantia has not yet had a Trinity Teacher Son.

> "The Sons of the next order to arrive on the average evolutionary world are the Trinity Teacher Sons, the divine Sons of the Paradise Trinity. Again we find Urantia out of step with its sister spheres in that your Jesus has promised to return. That promise he will certainly fulfill, but no one knows whether his second coming will precede or follow the appearances of Magisterial or Teacher Sons on Urantia." P52,S7,PP1,PG598

> "The revelation of truth is now extended to the central universe and to Paradise. The races are becoming highly spiritual. A great people has evolved and a great age is approaching. The educational, economic, and administrative systems of the planet are undergoing radical transformations. New values and relationships are being established. The kingdom of heaven is appearing on earth, and the glory of God is being shed abroad in the world." P52,S7,PP3,PG598

> "Life during this era is pleasant and profitable. Degeneracy and the antisocial end products of the long evolutionary struggle have been virtually obliterated. The length of life approaches five hundred Urantia years, and the reproductive rate of racial increase is intelligently controlled. An entirely new order of society has arrived. There are still great differences among mortals, but the state of society more nearly approaches the ideals of social brotherhood and spiritual equality. Representative government is vanishing, and the world is passing under the rule of individual self-control. The function of government is chiefly directed to collective tasks of social administration and economic co-ordination. The golden age is coming on apace; the temporal goal of the long and intense planetary evolutionary struggle is in sight. The reward of the ages is soon to be realized; the wisdom of the Gods is about to be manifested.
>
> The physical administration of a world during this age requires about one hour each day on the part of every adult individual; that is, the equivalent of one Urantia hour. The planet is in close touch with universe affairs, and its people scan the latest broadcasts with the same keen interest you now manifest in the latest editions of your daily newspapers. These races are occupied with a thousand things of interest unknown on your world." P52,S7,PP5,PG599

So there you have a glimpse of the average set of bestowal epochs or dispensations on an average inhabited world, along with comments about some differences that have occurred here on Urantia.

g. *What Happened Here on Earth*

What has happened here on Earth? There have been five bestowals so far:

1. The Planetary Prince. Ours joined a rebellion against God, and has been replaced in function.

2. Adam and Eve. Our Adam and Eve, our biologic uplifters, came to a rebellion-scarred planet. They had been instructed on how to proceed, but they defaulted. Their mission of biologic uplift was only partially successful.

3. Machiventa Melchizedek. An "emergency Son of world ministry" P93,S1,PP3,PG1014 who incarnated here to teach truth about God; to keep truth about God alive. This bestowal was not typical. Melchizedeks are an order of local universe Sons of God who's duties include emergency services. Machiventa Melchizedek is mentioned in the Bible, where he is called Melchizedek.

4. Jesus Christ, our Bestowal Son, who is our local universe Creator Son, a Paradise representative. And this bestowal came out of order.

5. *The Urantia Book*, a written revelation, also not typical.

To help with the following quote, Dalmatia was the material headquarters city established by the Planetary Prince and his staff some 500,000 years ago. Adam and Eve lived in the Garden of Eden about 38,000 years ago. Eden is named after Edentia, the capital world of the constellation to which our local system belongs. The following quote is *The Urantia Book's* summary of the five primary gifts we have received so far.

> "There have been many events of religious revelation but only five of epochal significance. These were as follows:
>
> 1. *The Dalamatian teachings.* The true concept of the First Source and Center was first promulgated on Urantia by the one hundred corporeal members of Prince Caligastia's staff. This expanding revelation of Deity went on for more than three hundred thousand years until it was suddenly terminated by the planetary secession and the disruption of the teaching regime. Except for the work of Van [a member of the corporeal staff who remained loyal to God during the rebellion], the influence of the Dalamatian revelation was practically lost to the whole world. Even the Nodites had forgotten this truth by the time of Adam's arrival. Of all who received the teachings of the one hundred, the red men held them longest, but the idea of the Great Spirit was but a hazy concept in Amerindian religion when contact with Christianity greatly clarified and strengthened it.
>
> 2. *The Edenic teachings.* Adam and Eve again portrayed the concept of the Father of all to the evolutionary peoples. The disruption of the first Eden halted the course of the Adamic revelation before it had ever fully started. But the aborted teachings of Adam were carried on by the Sethite priests, and some of these truths have never been entirely lost to the world. The entire trend of Levantine religious evolution was modified by the teachings of the Sethites. But by 2500 B.C. mankind had largely lost sight of the revelation sponsored in the days of Eden.
>
> 3. *Melchizedek of Salem.* This emergency Son of Nebadon inaugurated the third revelation of truth on Urantia. The cardinal precepts of his teachings were trust and faith. He taught trust in the omnipotent beneficence of God and proclaimed that faith was the act by which men earned God's favor. His teachings gradually commingled with the beliefs and practices of various evolutionary religions and finally developed into those theologic systems present on Urantia at the opening of the first millennium after Christ.
>
> 4. *Jesus of Nazareth.* Christ Michael presented for the fourth time to Urantia the concept of God as the Universal Father, and this teaching has generally persisted ever since. The essence of his teaching was love and service, the loving worship which a creature son voluntarily gives in recognition of, and response to, the loving ministry of God his

Father; the freewill service which such creature sons bestow upon their brethren in the joyous realization that in this service they are likewise serving God the Father.

5. *The Urantia Papers*. The papers, of which this is one, constitute the most recent presentation of truth to the mortals of Urantia. These papers differ from all previous revelations, for they are not the work of a single universe personality but a composite presentation by many beings. But no revelation short of the attainment of the Universal Father can ever be complete. All other celestial ministrations are no more than partial, transient, and practically adapted to local conditions in time and space. While such admissions as this may possibly detract from the immediate force and authority of all revelations, the time has arrived on Urantia when it is advisable to make such frank statements, even at the risk of weakening the future influence and authority of this, the most recent of the revelations of truth to the mortal races of Urantia." P92,S4,PP4,PG1007

CHAPTER 5: THE LUCIFER REBELLION, AND ADAM'S AND EVE'S DEFAULT

Beginning about 200,000 years ago, our planet became involved in, and has been scarred by, a rebellion against God.

a. *The Lucifer Rebellion in our Local System*

Lucifer was a brilliant local universe son of God (a Lanonandek), who was our System Sovereign. Our system includes 619 inhabited worlds.

In our local universe, which contains 10 million inhabited planets and 10,000 System Sovereigns, only three System Sovereigns have gone astray. Two of these, Lucifer and Satan, were in our local system.

> "Lucifer and his first assistant, Satan, had reigned on Jerusem for more than five hundred thousand years when in their hearts they began to array themselves against the Universal Father and his then vicegerent Son, Michael." P53,S2,PP1,PG602 [Jerusem is the headquarters world of our local system. Michael is our local universe Creator Son.]

> "Whatever the early origins of trouble in the hearts of Lucifer and Satan, the final outbreak took form as the Lucifer Declaration of Liberty." P53,S3,PP1,PG603

> "And it was with such a Declaration of Liberty that Lucifer launched his orgy of darkness and death." P53,S3,PP7,PG604

Among many other things, Lucifer declared that the Universal Father didn't really exist, and that reverence was ignorance. He championed individual self-assertion.

> "This "war in heaven" [on system headquarters] was not a physical battle as such a conflict might be conceived on Urantia. In the early days of the struggle Lucifer held forth continuously in the planetary amphitheater. Gabriel [Chief Executive of our local universe] conducted an unceasing exposure of the rebel sophistries from his headquarters taken up near at hand. The various personalities present on the sphere who were in doubt as to their attitude would journey back and forth between these discussions until they arrived at a final decision.
>
> But this war in heaven was very terrible and very real. While displaying none of the barbarities so characteristic of physical warfare on the immature worlds, this conflict was far more deadly; material life is in jeopardy in material combat, but the war in heaven was fought in terms of life eternal." P53,S5,PP6,PG606

> "At the outbreak of rebellion on Jerusem the head of the seraphic hosts joined the Lucifer cause. This no doubt explains why such a large number of the fourth order, the system administrator seraphim, went astray. The seraphic leader was spiritually

blinded by the brilliant personality of Lucifer; his charming ways fascinated the lower orders of celestial beings. They simply could not comprehend that it was possible for such a dazzling personality to go wrong." P53,S6,PP2,PG606

"The Lucifer rebellion was system wide. Thirty-seven seceding Planetary Princes swung their world administrations largely to the side of the archrebel. Only on Panoptia [another planet] did the Planetary Prince fail to carry his people with him. On this world, under the guidance of the Melchizedeks, the people rallied to the support of Michael. Ellanora, a young woman of that mortal realm, grasped the leadership of the human races, and not a single soul on that strife-torn world enlisted under the Lucifer banner." P53,S7,PP1,PG607 [Thirty-seven planetary administrators, including ours, out of 619 in our local system, joined the rebellion. Melchizedeks are local universe Sons of God who, among other things, do emergency services. Michael is our local universe Creator Son.]

"Lucifer and Satan freely roamed the Satania system until the completion of the bestowal mission of Michael on Urantia. They were last on your world together during the time of their combined assault upon the Son of Man." P53,S8,PP1,PG609

"There was survival for mortals and security for angels when your Master, in reply to the Lucifer proposals, calmly and with divine assurance replied, "Get you behind me, Satan." That was, in principle, the real end of the Lucifer rebellion." P53,S8,PP4,PG609

"It is true that Satan did periodically visit Caligastia and others of the fallen princes right up to the time of the presentation of these revelations, when there occurred the first hearing of Gabriel's plea for the annihilation of the archrebels. Satan is now unqualifiedly detained on the Jerusem prison worlds." P53,S9,PP4,PG611

"The rebellion has ended on Jerusem. It ends on the fallen worlds as fast as divine Sons arrive. We believe that all rebels who will ever accept mercy have done so. We await the flashing broadcast that will deprive these traitors of personality existence. We anticipate the verdict of Uversa will be announced by the executionary broadcast which will effect the annihilation of these interned rebels. Then will you look for their places, but they shall not be found." P53,S9,PP7,PG611 [Uversa is the headquarters of our superuniverse.]

b. *The Rebellion on our Planet, and Some More Planetary History*

About 500,000 years ago, about one half billion primitive humans lived on Urantia "... well scattered over Europe, Asia, and Africa." P66,PP2,PG741 The various colored races had first made their appearance. At this time our Planetary Prince, Caligastia, arrived to administer the affairs of our planet.

"The Planetary Prince of Urantia was not sent out on his mission alone but was accompanied by the usual corps of assistants and administrative helpers.

At the head of this group was Daligastia, the associate-assistant of the Planetary Prince. Daligastia was also a secondary Lanonandek Son, being number 319,407 of that order. He ranked as an assistant at the time of his assignment as Caligastia's associate.

> The planetary staff included a large number of angelic co-operators and a host of other celestial beings assigned to advance the interests and promote the welfare of the human races. But from your standpoint the most interesting group of all were the corporeal members of the Prince's staff—sometimes referred to as *the Caligastia one hundred."* P66,S2,PP1,PG742 [The Caligastia 100 are discussed above, in Chapter 4.]

The Planetary Prince and his staff had set up a headquarters city which was situated in the "... Persian Gulf region of those days, in the district corresponding to later Mesopotamia". P66,S3,PP1,PG743 This city, Dalamatia, was set up to interface with the evolutionary humans, to teach them. This had all been going on according to plan for about 300,000 years, when our Planetary Prince, Caligastia, and his assistant, Daligastia, joined Lucifer's rebellion.

At the time of rebellion, about 200,000 years ago, there were different types of planetary inhabitants. These included humans, angels, the Planetary Prince and his assistant, the Caligastia 100 (the corporeal staff) and their 100 human assistants, midwayers, and others. In all these groups, some joined the rebellion, and some didn't.

Van, who was one of the 100 corporeal staff (one of the Caligastia one hundred), and his associate Amadon, remained loyal to God, and were the leaders of the resistance to the rebellion. These material superhumans had in their possession, and were sustained by, the tree of life. They lived here for 150,000 years, up until the time of Adam and Eve, about 38,000 years ago. The disloyal members of corporeal staff became mortal without the tree of life. The disloyal corporeal staff were nonetheless supermen and superwomen, and under their leader, Nod, started another race or culture called the Nodites. (The Bible makes reference to the Nodites when it mentions that Cain slew Abel and went off to live in the land of Nod.)

> "Very little was heard of Lucifer on Urantia owing to the fact that he assigned his first lieutenant, Satan, to advocate his cause on your planet. Satan ... entered fully into the Lucifer insurrection. The "devil" is none other than Caligastia, the deposed Planetary Prince of Urantia and a Son of the secondary order of Lanonandeks. At the time Michael was on Urantia in the flesh, Lucifer, Satan, and Caligastia were leagued together to effect the miscarriage of his bestowal mission. But they signally failed." P53,S1,PP4,PG602

> "The majority of the primary midwayers went into sin at the time of the Lucifer rebellion. When the devastation of the planetary rebellion was reckoned up, among other losses it was discovered that of the original 50,000, 40,119 had joined the Caligastia secession.
> The original number of secondary midwayers was 1,984, and of these 873 failed to align themselves with the rule of Michael and were duly interned in connection with the planetary adjudication of Urantia on the day of Pentecost. No one can forecast the future of these fallen creatures." P77,S7,PP1,PG863 [Secondary midwayers came into being during the times of Adam and Eve. Adams first son, Adamson, married a pure line descendant of the corporeal staff, and the secondary midwayers came into being through sex unions of certain special offspring of these two superhumans.]

> "On Urantia forty members of the corporeal staff of one hundred (including Van) refused to join the insurrection. Many of the staff's human assistants (modified and otherwise) were also brave and noble defenders of Michael and his universe government.

There was a terrible loss of personalities among seraphim and cherubim. Almost one half of the administrator and transition seraphim assigned to the planet joined their leader and Daligastia in support of the cause of Lucifer." P67,S3,PP2,PG756

"Abaddon was the chief of the staff of Caligastia. He followed his master into rebellion and has ever since acted as chief executive of the Urantia rebels. Beelzebub was the leader of the disloyal midway creatures who allied themselves with the forces of the traitorous Caligastia." P53,S1,PP5,PG602

"Both groups of rebel midwayers are now held in custody awaiting the final adjudication of the affairs of the system rebellion. But they did many strange things on earth prior to the inauguration of the present planetary dispensation.

These disloyal midwayers were able to reveal themselves to mortal eyes under certain circumstances, and especially was this true of the associates of Beelzebub, the leader of the apostate secondary midwayers. But these unique creatures must not be confused with certain of the rebel cherubim and seraphim who also were on earth up to the time of Christ's death and resurrection. Some of the older writers designated these rebellious midway creatures as evil spirits and demons, and the apostate seraphim as evil angels." P77,S7,PP3,PG863

While Jesus (Michael of Nebadon) walked the Earth, and met Lucifer, Satan, and Calagastia, he actually was dealing with his own rebellious offspring. By the time he met them, he had become fully aware of who he was, his human incarnation had been approved by the Universal Father, he had gained full Sovereignty over his local universe, and he technically terminated the rebellion on this planet.

"To the many proposals and counterproposals of the emissaries of Lucifer, Jesus only made reply: "May the will of my Paradise Father prevail, and you, my rebellious son, may the Ancients of Days judge you divinely. I am your Creator-father; I can hardly judge you justly, and my mercy you have already spurned. I commit you to the adjudication of the Judges of a greater universe." PP134,S8,PP7,PG1493 [Ancients of Days are superuniverse-level judges.]

Up until the time of Jesus, some of the rebellious midwayers and angels could enter or possess weaker human minds.

"On no world can evil spirits possess any mortal mind subsequent to the life of a Paradise bestowal Son. But before the days of Christ Michael on Urantia- before the universal coming of the Thought Adjusters and the pouring out of the Master's spirit upon all flesh-these rebel midwayers were actually able to influence the minds of certain inferior mortals and somewhat to control their actions." P77,S7,PP5,PG863

"Even prior to Pentecost no rebel spirit could dominate a normal human mind, and since that day even the weak minds of inferior mortals are free from such possibilities. The supposed casting out of devils since the arrival of the Spirit of Truth has been a matter of confounding a belief in demoniacal possession with hysteria, insanity, and feeble-mindedness. But just because Michael's bestowal has forever liberated all human minds on Urantia from the possibility of demoniacal possession, do not imagine that such was not a reality in former ages." P77,S7,PP6,PG863

However:

> "The last act of Michael before leaving Urantia was to offer mercy to Caligastia and Daligastia [our rebellious Planetary Prince and his assistant], but they spurned his tender proffer. Caligastia, your apostate Planetary Prince, is still free on Urantia to prosecute his nefarious designs, but he has absolutely no power to enter the minds of men, neither can he draw near to their souls to tempt or corrupt them unless they really desire to be cursed with his wicked presence." P53,S8,PP6,PG610

So, until Caligastia has been adjudicated/incarcerated, there really is a "devil" that humans can contact, to their detriment, if they really want to.

> "In general, when weak and dissolute mortals are supposed to be under the influence of devils and demons, they are merely being dominated by their own inherent and debased tendencies, being led away by their own natural propensities. The devil has been given a great deal of credit for evil which does not belong to him. Caligastia has been comparatively impotent since the cross of Christ." P53,S8,PP9,PG610

Up until the rebellion, our planet was on communication or broadcast circuits in our local universe. At the outbreak of the rebellion, we and our local system were isolated. These communication links were shut off. (This does not mean that we were isolated from God's ministries, but we were/are isolated from broadcast services.)

> "The system circuits will not be reinstated so long as Lucifer lives." P53,S9,PP6,PG611

c. *Adam and Eve's Default*

Adam and Eve were our biologic uplifters, as discussed in the previous chapter. Adam and Eve's default is related to the rebellion, in that Eve initiated the default upon succumbing to a plot by the traitorous Caligastia, even though Adam and Eve had been thoroughly briefed beforehand.

> "These Sons [Adam and Eve] are the material gift of the Creator Son to the inhabited worlds. Together with the Planetary Prince, they remain on their planet of assignment throughout the evolutionary course of such a sphere. Such an adventure on a world having a Planetary Prince is not much of a hazard, but on an apostate planet, a realm without a spiritual ruler and deprived of interplanetary communication, such a mission is fraught with grave danger." P51,PP2,PG580

> "Probably no Material Sons of Nebadon were ever faced with such a difficult and seemingly hopeless task as confronted Adam and Eve in the sorry plight of Urantia. But they would have sometime met with success had they been more farseeing and *patient*. Both of them, especially Eve, were altogether too impatient; they were not willing to settle down to the long, long endurance test. They wanted to see some immediate results, and they did, but the results thus secured proved most disastrous both to themselves and to their world." P75,S1,PP6,PG840

> "The traitorous Planetary Prince did succeed in compromising your Adam and Eve, but he failed in his effort to involve them in the Lucifer rebellion." P51,S3,PP4,PG583

"But the fallen Prince was persistent and determined. He soon gave up working on Adam and decided to try a wily flank attack on Eve. The evil one concluded that the only hope for success lay in the adroit employment of suitable persons belonging to the upper strata of the Nodite group, the descendants of his onetime corporeal-staff associates. And the plans were accordingly laid for entrapping the mother of the violet race.

It was farthest from Eve's intention ever to do anything which would militate against Adam's plans or jeopardize their planetary trust. Knowing the tendency of woman to look upon immediate results rather than to plan farsightedly for more remote effects, the Melchizedeks, before departing, had especially enjoined Eve as to the peculiar dangers besetting their isolated position on the planet and had in particular warned her never to stray from the side of her mate, that is, to attempt no personal or secret methods of furthering their mutual undertakings. Eve had most scrupulously carried out these instructions for more than one hundred years, and it did not occur to her that any danger would attach to the increasingly private and confidential visits she was enjoying with a certain Nodite leader named Serapatatia. The whole affair developed so gradually and naturally that she was taken unawares." P75,S2,PP3,PG840

"Serapatatia became one of the most able and efficient of all of Adam's lieutenants. He was entirely honest and thoroughly sincere in all of his activities; he was never conscious, even later on, that he was being used as a circumstantial tool of the wily Caligastia." P75,S3,PP3,PG841

"He held many conferences with Adam and Eve— especially with Eve—and they talked over many plans for improving their methods. One day, during a talk with Eve, it occurred to Serapatatia that it would be very helpful if, while awaiting the recruiting of large numbers of the violet race, something could be done in the meantime immediately to advance the needy waiting tribes. Serapatatia contended that, if the Nodites, as the most progressive and cooperative race, could have a leader born to them of part origin in the violet stock, it would constitute a powerful tie binding these peoples more closely to the Garden. And all of this was soberly and honestly considered to be for the good of the world since this child, to be reared and educated in the Garden, would exert a great influence for good over his father's people.

It should again be emphasized that Serapatatia was altogether honest and wholly sincere in all that he proposed. He never once suspected that he was playing into the hands of Caligastia and Daligastia. Serapatatia was entirely loyal to the plan of building up a strong reserve of the violet race before attempting the world-wide upstepping of the confused peoples of Urantia. But this would require hundreds of years to consummate, and he was impatient; he wanted to see some immediate results—something in his own lifetime. He made it clear to Eve that Adam was oftentimes discouraged by the little that had been accomplished toward uplifting the world.

For more than five years these plans were secretly matured. At last they had developed to the point where Eve consented to have a secret conference with Cano, the most brilliant mind and active leader of the near-by colony of friendly Nodites. Cano was very sympathetic with the Adamic regime; in fact, he was the sincere spiritual leader of those neighboring Nodites who favored friendly relations with the Garden.

The fateful meeting occurred during the twilight hours of the autumn evening, not far from the home of Adam. Eve had never before met the beautiful and enthusiastic Cano—and he was a magnificent specimen of the survival of the superior physique and outstanding intellect of his remote progenitors of the Prince's staff. And Cano also thoroughly believed in the righteousness of the Serapatatia project. (Outside of the Garden, multiple mating was a common practice.)

Influenced by flattery, enthusiasm, and great personal persuasion, Eve then and there consented to embark upon the much-discussed enterprise, to add her own little scheme of world saving to the larger and more far-reaching divine plan. Before she quite realized what was transpiring, the fatal step had been taken. It was done." P75,S3,PP5,PG841

"And as the Material Son and Daughter thus communed in the moonlit Garden, "the voice in the Garden" reproved them for disobedience. And that voice was none other than my own announcement to the Edenic pair that they had transgressed the Garden covenant; that they had disobeyed the instructions of the Melchizedeks; that they had defaulted in the execution of their oaths of trust to the sovereign of the universe." P75,S4,PP2,PG842 [The two papers in *The Urantia Book* from which these Adam and Eve quotes were taken were narrated and presented by Solonia, the seraphic (angelic) "voice in the Garden."]

"Even though this project of modifying the divine plan had been conceived and executed with entire sincerity and with only the highest motives concerning the welfare of the world, it constituted evil because it represented the wrong way to achieve righteous ends, because it departed from the right way, the divine plan." P75,S4,PP7,PG842

"Eve's disillusionment was truly pathetic. Adam discerned the whole predicament and, while heartbroken and dejected, entertained only pity and sympathy for his erring mate.

It was in the despair of the realization of failure that Adam, the day after Eve's misstep, sought out Laotta, the brilliant Nodite woman who was head of the western schools of the Garden, and with premeditation committed the folly of Eve. But do not misunderstand; Adam was not beguiled; he knew exactly what he was about; he deliberately chose to share the fate of Eve. He loved his mate with a supermortal affection, and the thought of the possibility of a lonely vigil on Urantia without her was more than he could endure.

When they learned what had happened to Eve, the infuriated inhabitants of the Garden became unmanageable; they declared war on the near-by Nodite settlement. They swept out through the gates of Eden and down upon these unprepared people, utterly destroying them—not a man, woman, or child was spared. And Cano, the father of Cain yet unborn, also perished.

Upon the realization of what had happened, Serapatatia was overcome with consternation and beside himself with fear and remorse. The next day he drowned himself in the great river." P75,S5,PP4,PG843

Adam and Eve's group left the first garden to avoid being wiped out by revengeful Nodites.

"All in all, there probably never was a more disheartening miscarriage of wisdom on any planet in all Nebadon. But it is not surprising that these missteps occur in the affairs of the evolutionary universes. We are a part of a gigantic creation, and it is not strange that everything does not work in perfection; our universe was not created in perfection. Perfection is our eternal goal, not our origin." P75,S8,PP6,PG846

d. *A Positive Result of the Rebellion and the Default*

"Misfortune has not, however, been the sole lot of Urantia; this planet has also been the most fortunate in the local universe of Nebadon. Urantians should count it all gain if the blunders of their ancestors and the mistakes of their early world rulers so plunged the planet into such a hopeless state of confusion, all the more confounded by evil and sin, that this very background of darkness should so appeal to Michael of Nebadon [Jesus] that he selected this world as the arena wherein to reveal the loving personality of the Father in heaven. It is not that Urantia needed a Creator Son to set its tangled affairs in order; it is rather that the evil and sin on Urantia afforded the Creator Son a more striking background against which to reveal the matchless love, mercy, and patience of the Paradise Father." P76,S5,PP7,PG853

CHAPTER 6: WOMEN, MEN, EQUALITY, MARRIAGE, AND FAMILY

The success of civilization, and some of life's highest meanings and values, are dependent on or related to family life. Women and men are equal before God, and there are feminine attributes of God. And in spite of inherent sex equality, gender discrimination can and does occur among humans, especially in earlier stages of planetary development.

a. *Feminine Attributes of God*

"When a Creator Son departs from Paradise to embark upon the adventure of universe making, to become the head—virtually the God—of the local universe of his own organization, then, for the first time, he finds himself in intimate contact with, and in many respects dependent upon, the Third Source and Center. The Infinite Spirit, though abiding with the Father and the Son at the center of all things, is destined to function as the actual and effective helper of each Creator Son. Therefore is each Creator Son accompanied by a Creative Daughter of the Infinite Spirit, that being who is destined to become the Divine Minister, the Mother Spirit of the new local universe." P21,S2,PP2,PG235

"On that occasion, before the assembled administrators of the universe, the triumphant Creator Son elevates the Universe Mother Spirit to cosovereignty and acknowledges the Spirit consort as his equal." P17,S6,PP8,PG204

"... while the Universe Mother Spirit concurrently engages in her initial solitary effort at spirit reproduction. Thus begins the creation of the seraphic hosts of a local universe." P38,S1,PP1,PG418

I suspect that Divinity transcends male and female. *The Urantia Book* refers to offspring of the Paradise Infinite Spirit, such as the local universe Mother Spirit, and angels, in the feminine, while referring to the Father, Sons, and the Paradise Infinite Spirit, in the masculine. Yet, to distinguish a qualitative difference between the love of the Father and the love of the Eternal Son, *The Urantia Book* says:

"As love is comprehended on a sex planet, the love of God is more comparable to the love of a father, while the love of the Eternal Son is more like the affection of a mother. Crude, indeed, are such illustrations, but I employ them in the hope of conveying to the human mind the thought that there is a difference, not in divine content but in quality and technique of expression, between the love of the Father and the love of the Son." P6,S3,PP5,P76

"In the same sense that God is the Universal Father, the Son is the Universal Mother. And all of us, high and low, constitute their universal family. P6,S8,PP1,PG79

b. Men, Women, and Equality

"Young are usually born singly, multiple births being the exception, and the family life is fairly uniform on all types of planets. Sex equality prevails on all advanced worlds; male and female are equal in mind endowment and spiritual status. We do not regard a planet as having emerged from barbarism so long as one sex seeks to tyrannize over the other." P49,S4,PP4,PG564

"On some planets the male may rule the female; on others the reverse prevails." P52,S2,PP7,PG591 [During earlier stages of planetary development.]

"Hunger, vanity, and ghost fear were continuous in their social pressure, but sex gratification was transient and spasmodic. The sex urge alone did not impel primitive men and women to assume the heavy burdens of home maintenance. The early home was founded upon the sex restlessness of the male when deprived of frequent gratification and upon that devoted mother love of the human female, which in measure she shares with the females of all the higher animals. The presence of a helpless baby determined the early differentiation of male and female activities; the woman had to maintain a settled residence where she could cultivate the soil. And from earliest times, where woman was has always been regarded as the home." P68,S2,PP6,PG765

"Woman's work was derived from the selective presence of the child; women naturally love babies more than men do. Thus woman became the routine worker, while man became the hunter and fighter, engaging in accentuated periods of work and rest.
All down through the ages the taboos have operated to keep woman strictly in her own field. Man has most selfishly chosen the more agreeable work, leaving the routine drudgery to woman. Man has always been ashamed to do woman's work, but woman has never shown any reluctance to doing man's work. But strange to record, both men and women have always worked together in building and furnishing the home." P69,S3,PP2,PG774

"Among the more advanced races, women are not so large or so strong as men. Woman, being the weaker, therefore became the more tactful; she early learned to trade upon her sex charms. She became more alert and conservative than man, though slightly less profound. Man was woman's superior on the battlefield and in the hunt; but at home woman has usually outgeneraled even the most primitive of men." P84,S3,PP5,PG934

"Herein has sex been the unrecognized and unsuspected civilizer of the savage; for this same sex impulse automatically and unerringly *compels man to think* and eventually *leads him to love.*" P83,PP3,PG922

"When man was a hunter, he was fairly kind to woman, but after the domestication of animals, coupled with the Caligastia confusion, many tribes shamefully treated their women. They treated them altogether too much as they treated their animals. Man's brutal treatment of woman constitutes one of the darkest chapters of human history. P69,S7,PP5,PG778 [Caligastia was our rebellious Planetary Prince.]

"The sexes have had great difficulty in understanding each other. Man found it hard to understand woman, regarding her with a strange mixture of ignorant mistrust and fearful fascination, if not with suspicion and contempt. Many tribal and racial traditions relegate trouble to Eve, Pandora, or some other representative of womankind. These narratives were always distorted so as to make it appear that the woman brought evil upon man; and all this indicates the onetime universal distrust of woman. Among the reasons cited in support of a celibate priesthood, the chief was the baseness of woman. The fact that most supposed witches were women did not improve the olden reputation of the sex." P84,S4,PP4,PG935

"The so-called modesty of women respecting their clothing and the exposure of the person grew out of the deadly fear of being observed at the time of a menstrual period. To be thus detected was a grievous sin, the violation of a taboo. Under the mores of olden times, every woman, from adolescence to the end of the childbearing period, was subjected to complete family and social quarantine one full week each month. Everything she might touch, sit upon, or lie upon was "defiled." It was for long the custom to brutally beat a girl after each monthly period in an effort to drive the evil spirit out of her body. But when a woman passed beyond the childbearing age, she was usually treated more considerately, being accorded more rights and privileges. In view of all this it was not strange that women were looked down upon. Even the Greeks held the menstruating woman as one of the three great causes of defilement, the other two being pork and garlic." P84,S4,PP8,PG936

"The modern idea of sex equality is beautiful and worthy of an expanding civilization, but it is not found in nature. When might is right, man lords it over woman; when more justice, peace, and fairness prevail, she gradually emerges from slavery and obscurity. Woman's social position has generally varied inversely with the degree of militarism in any nation or age." P84,S4,PP3,PG936

"The early Chinese and the Greeks treated women better than did most surrounding peoples. But the Hebrews were exceedingly distrustful of them. In the Occident woman has had a difficult climb under the Pauline doctrines which became attached to Christianity, although Christianity did advance the mores by imposing more stringent sex obligations upon man. Woman's estate is little short of hopeless under the peculiar degradation which attaches to her in Mohammedanism, and she fares even worse under the teachings of several other Oriental religions." P84,S5,PP6,PG937

"Woman is man's equal partner in race reproduction, hence just as important in the unfolding of racial evolution; therefore has evolution increasingly worked toward the realization of women's rights. But women's rights are by no means men's rights. Woman cannot thrive on man's rights any more than man can prosper on woman's rights.

Each sex has its own distinctive sphere of existence, together with its own rights within that sphere. If woman aspires literally to enjoy all of man's rights, then, sooner or later, pitiless and emotionless competition will certainly replace that chivalry and special consideration which many women now enjoy, and which they have so recently won from men.

Civilization never can obliterate the behavior gulf between the sexes. From age to age the mores change, but instinct never. Innate maternal affection will never permit emancipated woman to become man's serious rival in industry. Forever each sex will remain supreme in its own domain, domains determined by biologic differentiation and by mental dissimilarity.

Each sex will always have its own special sphere, albeit they will ever and anon overlap. Only socially will men and women compete on equal terms." P84,S5,PP11,PG938

"Male and female are, practically regarded, two distinct varieties of the same species living in close and intimate association. Their viewpoints and entire life reactions are essentially different; they are wholly incapable of full and real comprehension of each other. Complete understanding between the sexes is not attainable.

Women seem to have more intuition than men, but they also appear to be somewhat less logical. Woman, however, has always been the moral standard-bearer and the spiritual leader of mankind. The hand that rocks the cradle still fraternizes with destiny.

The differences of nature, reaction, viewpoint, and thinking between men and women, far from occasioning concern, should be regarded as highly beneficial to mankind, both individually and collectively. Many orders of universe creatures are created in dual phases of personality manifestation. ... Such dual associations greatly multiply versatility and overcome inherent limitations ..." P84,S6,PP3,PG938

"While the sexes never can hope fully to understand each other, they are effectively complementary..." P84,S6,PP7,PG939

"The most astonishing and the most revolutionary feature of Michael's mission on earth was his attitude toward women. In a day and generation when a man was not supposed to salute even his own wife in a public place, Jesus dared to take women along as teachers of the gospel in connection with his third tour of Galilee. And he had the consummate courage to do this in the face of the rabbinic teaching which declared that it was "better that the words of the law should be burned than delivered to women."" P149,S2,PP8,PG1671

"The apostles never ceased to be shocked by Jesus' willingness to talk with women, women of questionable character, even immoral women. It was very difficult for Jesus to teach his apostles that women, even so-called immoral women, have souls which can choose God as their Father, thereby becoming daughters of God and candidates for life everlasting. Even nineteen centuries later many show the same unwillingness to grasp the Master's teachings..." P143,S5,PP11,PG1614

"No longer can man presume to monopolize the ministry of religious service. The Pharisee might go on thanking god that he was "not born a woman, a leper, or a gentile," but among the followers of Jesus woman has been forever set free from all religious discriminations based on sex." P194,S3,PP14,PG2065

c. *Marriage and Family*

"Sex mating is instinctive, children are the natural result, and the family thus automatically comes into existence. As are the families of the race or nation, so is its society. If the families are good, the society is likewise good. The great cultural stability of the Jewish and of the Chinese peoples lies in the strength of their family groups.

Woman's instinct to love and care for children conspired to make her the interested party in promoting marriage and primitive family life. Man was only forced into home building by the pressure of the later mores and social conventions; he was slow to take an interest in the establishment of marriage and home because the sex act imposes no biologic consequences upon him." P85,S7,PP1,PG939

"The reproductive urge unfailingly brings men and women together for self-perpetuation but, alone, does not insure their remaining together in mutual cooperation — the founding of a home.

Every successful human institution embraces antagonisms of personal interest which have been adjusted to practical working harmony, and homemaking is no exception. Marriage, the basis of home building, is the highest manifestation of that antagonistic co-operation which so often characterizes the contacts of nature and society. The conflict is inevitable. Mating is inherent; it is natural. But marriage is not biologic; it is sociologic. Passion insures that man and woman will come together, but the weaker parental instinct and the social mores hold them together." P84,S6,PP1,PG938

"There always have been and always will be two distinct realms of marriage: the mores, the laws regulating the external aspects of mating, and the otherwise secret and personal relations of men and women. Always has the individual been rebellious against the sex regulations imposed by society; and this is the reason for this agelong sex problem: Self-maintenance is individual but is carried on by the group; self-perpetuation is social but is secured by individual impulse." P82,S3,PP2,PG915

"Ideal marriage must be founded on something more stable than the fluctuations of sentiment and the fickleness of mere sex attraction; it must be based on genuine and mutual personal devotion. And thus, if you can build up such trustworthy and effective small units of human association, when these are assembled in the aggregate, the world will behold a great and glorified social structure, the civilization of mortal maturity." P160,S4,PP4,PG1777 [From a discourse by Rodan of Alexandria.]

Jesus "... exalted marriage as the most ideal and highest of all human relationships. Likewise, he intimated strong disapproval of the lax and unfair divorce practices of the Jerusalem Jews, who at that time permitted a man to divorce his wife for the most trifling of reasons, such as being a poor cook, a faulty housekeeper, or for no better reason than that he had become enamoured of a better-looking woman.

"... And so, while Jesus refused to make pronouncements dealing with marriage and divorce, he did most bitterly denounce these shameful floutings of the marriage relationship and pointed out their injustice to women and children. He never sanctioned any divorce practice which gave man any advantage over woman; the Master countenanced only those teachings which accorded women equality with men." P167,S5,PP3,PG1838

"Marriage, with children and consequent family life, is stimulative of the highest potentials in human nature and simultaneously provides the ideal avenue for the expression of these quickened attributes of mortal personality. The family provides for the biologic perpetuation of the human species. The home is the natural social arena wherein the ethics of blood brotherhood may be grasped by the growing children. The family is the fundamental unit of fraternity in which parents and children learn those lessons of patience, altruism, tolerance, and forbearance which are so essential to the realization of brotherhood among all men." P84,S7,PP18,PG941

"And then, in bidding him farewell, Jesus said: "My brother, always remember that man has no rightful authority over woman unless the woman has willingly and voluntarily given him such authority. Your wife has engaged to go through life with you, to help you fight its battles, and to assume the far greater share of the burden of bearing and rearing your children; and in return for this special service it is only fair that she receive from you that special protection which man can give to woman as the partner who must carry, bear, and nurture the children. The loving care and consideration which a man is willing to bestow upon his wife and their children are the measure of that man's attainment of the higher levels of creative and spiritual self-consciousness. ..."" P133,S2,PP2,PG1471

"... but this same Father has directed the creation of male and female, and it is the divine will that men and women should find their highest service and consequent joy in the establishment of homes for the reception and training of children, in the creation of whom these parents become copartners with the Makers of heaven and earth." P167,S5,PP7,PG1839 [Jesus speaking.]

CHAPTER 7: RELIGION

a. *Types of Religion*

One of the adjutant mind spirits (explained in Chapter 10) is the Spirit of Worship, which creates a religious impulse in humans. This brings forth natural or evolutionary religion. And from time to time, truth is revealed to humans. In society, religion originating from both of these sources tends to become ordered and established.

> "While the religions of the world have a double origin—natural and revelatory—at any one time and among any one people there are to be found three distinct forms of religious devotion. And these three manifestations of the religious urge are:
>
> 1. *Primitive religion.* The seminatural and instinctive urge to fear mysterious energies and worship superior forces, chiefly a religion of the physical nature, the religion of fear.
>
> 2. *The religion of civilization.* The advancing religious concepts and practices of the civilizing races—the religion of the mind—the intellectual theology of the authority of established religious tradition.
>
> 3. *True religion—the religion of revelation.* The revelation of supernatural values, a partial insight into eternal realities, a glimpse of the goodness and beauty of the infinite character of the Father in heaven—the religion of the spirit as demonstrated in human experience." P155,S5,PP2,PG1728

Some characteristics of religion spring from the early roots of fear and magic.

> "The people of Urantia continue to suffer from the influence of primitive concepts of God. The gods who go on a rampage in the storm; who shake the earth in their wrath and strike down men in their anger; who inflict their judgments of displeasure in times of famine and flood—these are the gods of primitive religion; they are not the Gods who live and rule the universes. Such concepts are a relic of the times when men supposed that the universe was under the guidance and domination of the whims of such imaginary gods. But mortal man is beginning to realize that he lives in a realm of comparative law and order as far as concerns the administrative policies and conduct of the Supreme Creators and the Supreme Controllers.
>
> The barbarous idea of appeasing an angry God, of propitiating an offended Lord, of winning the favor of Deity through sacrifices and penance and even by the shedding of blood, represents a religion wholly puerile and primitive, a philosophy unworthy of an enlightened age of science and truth. Such beliefs are utterly repulsive to the celestial beings and the divine rulers who serve and reign in the universes. It is an affront to God

to believe, hold, or teach that innocent blood must be shed in order to win his favor or to divert the fictitious divine wrath." P4,S5,PP3,PG60

"Religion has always been largely a matter of rites, rituals, observances, ceremonies, and dogmas. It has usually become tainted with that persistently mischief-making error, the chosen-people delusion. The cardinal religious ideas of incantation, inspiration, revelation, propitiation, repentance, atonement, intercession, sacrifice, prayer, confession, worship, survival after death, sacrament, ritual, ransom, salvation, redemption, covenant, uncleanness, purification, prophecy, original sin-they all go back to the early times of primordial ghost fear." P92,S3,PP2,PG1005

"Religion arises as a biologic reaction of mind to spiritual beliefs and the environment; it is the last thing to perish or change in a race. Religion is society's adjustment, in any age, to that which is mysterious. As a social institution it embraces rites, symbols, cults, scriptures, altars, shrines, and temples. Holy water, relics, fetishes, charms, vestments, bells, drums, and priesthoods are common to all religions. And it is impossible entirely to divorce purely evolved religion from either magic or sorcery." PP92,S1,PP3,PG1004

b. *Religions of Authority/Religions of Spirit*

"Until the races become highly intelligent and more fully civilized, there will persist many of those childlike and superstitious ceremonies which are so characteristic of the evolutionary religious practices of primitive and backward peoples. Until the human race progresses to the level of a higher and more general recognition of the realities of spiritual experience, large numbers of men and women will continue to show a personal preference for those religions of authority which require only intellectual assent, in contrast to the religion of the spirit, which entails active participation of mind and soul in the faith adventure of grappling with the rigorous realities of progressive human experience." P155,S5,PP8,PG1729 [Jesus speaking.]

"While the religion of authority may impart a present feeling of settled security, you pay for such a transient satisfaction the price of the loss of your spiritual freedom and religious liberty. My Father does not require of you as the price of entering the kingdom of heaven that you should force yourself to subscribe to a belief in things which are spiritually repugnant, unholy, and untruthful. It is not required of you that your own sense of mercy, justice, and truth should be outraged by submission to an outworn system of religious forms and ceremonies. The religion of the spirit leaves you forever free to follow the truth wherever the leadings of the spirit may take you. And who can judge—perhaps this spirit may have something to impart to this generation which other generations have refused to hear?" P155,S6,PP5,PG1731 [Jesus speaking.]

"The religions of authority can only divide men and set them in conscientious array against each other; the religion of the spirit will progressively draw men together and cause them to become understandingly sympathetic with one another." P155,S6,PP9,PG1732 [Jesus speaking.]

"Jesus made it clear that the great difference between the religion of the mind and the religion of the spirit is that, while the former is upheld by ecclesiastical authority, the latter is wholly based on human experience." P155,S5,PP11,PG1729

c. ***Erroneous Scripture Concepts***

"In his early teachings, Moses very wisely did not attempt to go back of Adam's time, and since Moses was the supreme teacher of the Hebrews, the stories of Adam became intimately associated with those of creation. That the earlier traditions recognized pre-Adamic civilization is clearly shown by the fact that later editors, intending to eradicate all reference to human affairs before Adam's time, neglected to remove the telltale reference to Cain's emigration to the "land of Nod," where he took himself a wife." P74,S8,PP8,PG837

"The Christian teachers perpetuated the belief in the fiat creation of the human race, and all this led directly to the formation of the hypothesis of a one-time golden age of utopian bliss and the theory of the fall of man or superman which accounted for the nonutopian condition of society. These outlooks on life and man's place in the universe were at best discouraging since they were predicated upon a belief in retrogression rather than progression, as well as implying a vengeful Deity, who had vented wrath upon the human race in retribution for the errors of certain onetime planetary administrators." P74,S8,PP13,PG838

"The ancient social brotherhoods were based on the rite of blood drinking; the early Jewish fraternity was a sacrificial blood affair. Paul started out to build a new Christian cult on "the blood of the everlasting covenant." And while he may have unnecessarily encumbered Christianity with teachings about blood and sacrifice, he did once and for all make an end of the doctrines of redemption through human or animal sacrifices. His theologic compromises indicate that even revelation must submit to the graduated control of evolution. According to Paul, Christ became the last and all-sufficient human sacrifice; the divine Judge is now fully and forever satisfied." P89,S9,PP3,PG984

"It was only natural that the cult of renunciation and humiliation should have paid attention to sexual gratification. The continence cult originated as a ritual among soldiers prior to engaging in battle; in later days it became the practice of "saints." This cult tolerated marriage only as an evil lesser than fornication. Many of the world's great religions have been adversely influenced by this ancient cult, but none more markedly than Christianity. The Apostle Paul was a devotee of this cult, and his personal views are reflected in the teachings which he fastened onto Christian theology: "It is good for a man not to touch a woman." "I would that all men were even as I myself." "I say, therefore, to the unmarried and widows, it is good for them to abide even as I." Paul well knew that such teachings were not a part of Jesus' gospel, and his acknowledgment of this is illustrated by his statement, "I speak this by permission and not by commandment." But this cult led Paul to look down upon women. And the pity of it all is that his personal opinions have long influenced the teachings of a great world religion. If the advice of the tentmaker-teacher were to be literally and universally obeyed, then would the human race come to a sudden and inglorious end. Furthermore, the involvement of a religion with the ancient continence cult leads directly to a war against marriage and the home, society's veritable foundation and the basic institution of human progress. And it is not to be wondered at that all such beliefs fostered the formation of celibate priesthoods in the many religions of various peoples." P89,S3,PP6,PG977

Chapter 7

"The Apostle Paul, in his efforts to bring the teachings of Jesus to the favorable notice of certain groups in his day, wrote many letters of instruction and admonition. Other teachers of Jesus' gospel did likewise, but none of them realized that some of these writings would subsequently be brought together by those who would set them forth as the embodiment of the teachings of Jesus. And so, while so-called Christianity does contain more of the Master's gospel than any other religion, it does also contain much that Jesus did not teach. Aside from the incorporation of many teachings from the Persian mysteries and much of the Greek philosophy into early Christianity, two great mistakes were made:

1. The effort to connect the gospel teaching directly onto the Jewish theology, as illustrated by the Christian doctrines of the atonement—the teaching that Jesus was the sacrificed Son who would satisfy the Father's stern justice and appease the divine wrath. These teachings originated in a praiseworthy effort to make the gospel of the kingdom more acceptable to disbelieving Jews. Though these efforts failed as far as winning the Jews was concerned, they did not fail to confuse and alienate many honest souls in all subsequent generations.

2. The second great blunder of the Master's early followers, and one which all subsequent generations have persisted in perpetuating, was to organize the Christian teaching so completely about the *person* of Jesus. This overemphasis of the personality of Jesus in the theology of Christianity has worked to obscure his teachings, and all of this has made it increasingly difficult for Jews, Mohammedans, Hindus, and other Eastern religionists to accept the teachings of Jesus. We would not belittle the place of the person of Jesus in a religion which might bear his name, but we would not permit such consideration to eclipse his inspired life or to supplant his saving message: the fatherhood of God and the brotherhood of man." P149,S2,PP2,PG1670

"The Christian religion is the religion about the life and teachings of Christ based upon the theology of Judaism, modified further through the assimilation of certain Zoroastrian teachings and Greek philosophy, and formulated primarily by three individuals: Philo, Peter, and Paul. It has passed through many phases of evolution since the time of Paul and has become so thoroughly Occidentalized that many non-European peoples very naturally look upon Christianity as a strange revelation of a strange God and for strangers." P92,S6,PP7,PG1011

"But great sorrow later attended the misinterpretation of the Master's inferences regarding prayer. There would have been little difficulty about these teachings if his exact words had been remembered and subsequently truthfully recorded. But as the record was made, believers eventually regarded prayer in Jesus' name as a sort of supreme magic, thinking that they would receive from the Father anything they asked for. For centuries honest souls have continued to wreck their faith against this stumbling block. How long will it take the world of believers to understand that prayer is not a process of getting your way but rather a program of taking God's way, an experience of learning how to recognize and execute the Father's will? It is entirely true that, when your will has been truly aligned with his, you can ask anything conceived by that will-union, and it will be granted. And such a will-union is effected by and through Jesus even as the life of the vine flows into and through the living branches."
P180,S2,PP3,PG1946

> "When once you grasp the idea of God as a true and loving Father, the only concept which Jesus ever taught, you must forthwith, in all consistency, utterly abandon all those primitive notions about God as an offended monarch, a stern and all-powerful ruler whose chief delight is to detect his subjects in wrongdoing and to see that they are adequately punished, unless some being almost equal to himself should volunteer to suffer for them, to die as a substitute and in their stead. The whole idea of ransom and atonement is incompatible with the concept of God as it was taught and exemplified by Jesus of Nazareth. The infinite love of God is not secondary to anything in the divine nature." P188,S4,PP8,PG2017

And the following two quotes are Jesus answering a question by Apostle Nathaniel about Scriptures.

> "These writings are the work of men, some of them holy men, others not so holy. The teachings of these books represent the views and extent of enlightenment of the times in which they had their origin. As a revelation of truth, the last are more dependable than the first. The Scriptures are faulty and altogether human in origin, but mistake not, they do constitute the best collection of religious wisdom and spiritual truth to be found in all the world at this time." P159,S4,PP3,PG1767

> "The thing most deplorable is not merely this erroneous idea of the absolute perfection of the Scripture record and the infallibility of its teachings, but rather the confusing misinterpretation of these sacred writings by the tradition-enslaved scribes and Pharisees at Jerusalem. And now will they employ both the doctrine of the inspiration of the Scriptures and their misinterpretations thereof in their determined effort to withstand these newer teachings of the gospel of the kingdom. Nathaniel, never forget, the Father does not limit the revelation of truth to any one generation or to any one people. Many earnest seekers after the truth have been, and will continue to be, confused and disheartened by these doctrines of the perfection of the Scriptures." P159,S4,PP6,PG1768

d. *Science, Secularism, Mechanistic Universe*

> "In reality, true religion cannot become involved in any controversy with science; it is in no way concerned with material things. Religion is simply indifferent to, but sympathetic with, science, while it supremely concerns itself with the *scientist*." P195,S6,PP2,PG2076

> "This profound experience of the reality of the divine indwelling forever transcends the crude materialistic technique of the physical sciences. You cannot put spiritual joy under a microscope; you cannot weigh love in a balance; you cannot measure moral values; neither can you estimate the quality of spiritual worship." P196,S3,PP15,PG2095

> "Secularism can never bring peace to mankind. Nothing can take the place of God in human society. But mark you well! Do not be quick to surrender the beneficent gains of the secular revolt from ecclesiastical totalitarianism. Western civilization today enjoys many liberties and satisfactions as a result of the secular revolt. The great mistake of secularism was this: In revolting against the almost total control of life by religious authority, and after attaining the liberation from such ecclesiastical tyranny, the secularists

went on to institute a revolt against God himself, sometimes tacitly and sometimes openly." P195,S8,PP6,PG2081

"Without God, without religion, scientific secularism can never co-ordinate its forces, harmonize its divergent and rivalrous interests, races, and nationalisms. This secularistic human society, notwithstanding its unparalleled materialistic achievement, is slowly disintegrating. The chief cohesive force resisting this disintegration of antagonism is nationalism. And nationalism is the chief barrier to world peace.

The inherent weakness of secularism is that it discards ethics and religion for politics and power. You simply cannot establish the brotherhood of men while ignoring or denying the fatherhood of God." P195,S8,PP10,PG2082

"The more of science you know, the less sure you can be; the more of religion you have, the more certain you are." P102,S1,PP3,PG1119

"If the universe were only material and man only a machine, there would be no science to embolden the scientist to postulate this mechanization of the universe. Machines cannot measure, classify, nor evaluate themselves. Such a scientific piece of work could be executed only by some entity of supermachine status.

If universe reality is only one vast machine, then man must be outside of the universe and apart from it in order to recognize such a fact and become conscious of the insight of such an evaluation." P195,S7,PP11,PG2079

e. *Social Religious Potential*

In some of the following quotes, *The Urantia Book* refers to Jesus and his teachings. Jesus' revelations or teachings are universe truths about God and love, for all of humanity, and are not partial to any one religion. Thus, the value of any religion becomes the degree to which it comprehends and lives the truth of the Creator, who is love. The value and power of *The Urantia Book*, in my opinion, are that it reveals basic universe truths of the divine and loving nature of the Creator.

"The many religions of Urantia are all good to the extent that they bring man to God and bring the realization of the Father to man. It is a fallacy for any group of religionists to conceive of their creed as *The Truth*; such attitudes bespeak more of theological arrogance than of certainty of faith. There is not a Urantia religion that could not profitably study and assimilate the best of the truths contained in every other faith, for all contain truth. Religionists would do better to borrow the best in their neighbors' living spiritual faith rather than to denounce the worst in their lingering superstitions and outworn rituals." P92,S7,PP3,PG1012

"Religious peace—brotherhood—can never exist unless all religions are willing to completely divest themselves of all ecclesiastical authority and fully surrender all concept of spiritual sovereignty. God alone is spirit sovereign." P134,S4,PP4,PG1487

"But paganized and socialized Christianity stands in need of new contact with the uncompromised teachings of Jesus; it languishes for lack of a new vision of the Master's life on earth. A new and fuller revelation of the religion of Jesus is destined to conquer an empire of materialistic secularism and to overthrow a world sway of mechanistic naturalism. Urantia is now quivering on the very brink of one of its most amazing and enthralling epochs of social readjustment, moral quickening, and spiritual enlightenment." P195,S9,PP2,PG2082

"The great hope of Urantia lies in the possibility of a new revelation of Jesus with a new and enlarged presentation of his saving message which would spiritually unite in loving service the numerous families of his present-day professed followers." P195,S10,PP16,PG2086

"Religion does need new leaders, spiritual men and women who will dare to depend solely on Jesus and his incomparable teachings." P195,S9,PP4,PG2082

"The brotherhood of man is, after all, predicated on the recognition of the fatherhood of God. The quickest way to realize the brotherhood of man on Urantia is to effect the spiritual transformation of present-day humanity. The only technique for accelerating the natural trend of social evolution is that of applying spiritual pressure from above, thus augmenting moral insight while enhancing the soul capacity of every mortal to understand and love every other mortal. Mutual understanding and fraternal love are transcendent civilizers and mighty factors in the world-wide realization of the brotherhood of man." P52,S6,PP7,PG598

f. *Religion and the Individual*

"Religion cannot be bestowed, received, loaned, learned, or lost. It is a personal experience which grows proportionally to the growing quest for final values. Cosmic growth thus attends on the accumulation of meanings and the ever-expanding elevation of values. But nobility itself is always an unconscious growth." P100,S1,PP7,PG1095

"Religion is man's supreme experience in the mortal nature, but finite language makes it forever impossible for theology ever adequately to depict real religious experience." P196,S3,PP25,PG2096

"Ever bear in mind—God and men need each other. They are mutually necessary to the full and final attainment of eternal personality experience in the divine destiny of universe finality."

"The kingdom of God is within you" was probably the greatest pronouncement Jesus ever made, next to the declaration that his Father is a living and loving spirit. P195,S10,PP3,PG2084

"When all is said and done, the Father idea is still the highest human concept of God." P196,S3,PP32,PG2097 [I imagine Divine Parent could be substituted for Father.]

"Never forget there is only one adventure which is more satisfying and thrilling than the attempt to discover the will of the living God, and that is the supreme experience of honestly trying to do that divine will. And fail not to remember that the will of God can be done in any earthly occupation. Some callings are not holy and others secular. All things are sacred in the lives of those who are spirit led; that is, subordinated to truth, ennobled by love, dominated by mercy, and restrained by fairness—justice. The spirit which my Father and I shall send into the world is not only the Spirit of Truth but also the spirit of idealistic beauty." P155,S6,PP10,PG1732 [Jesus, in a discourse on religion.]

g. *Prayer and Worship*

"Prayer is the breath of the spirit life in the midst of the material civilization of the races of mankind. Worship is salvation for the pleasure-seeking generations of mortals.
As prayer may be likened to recharging the spiritual batteries of the soul, so worship may be compared to the act of tuning in the soul to catch the universe broadcasts of the infinite spirit of the Universal Father." P144,S4,PP7,PG1621

"Worship is for its own sake; prayer embodies a self- or creature-interest element; that is the great difference between worship and prayer. ... We do not worship the Father because of anything we may derive from such veneration; we render such devotion and engage in such worship as a natural and spontaneous reaction to the recognition of the Father's matchless personality and because of his lovable nature and adorable attributes." P5,S3,PP3,PG65

"...while in true praying it is the sincere and trusting communication of the spiritual nature of the creature with the anywhere presence of the spirit of the Creator." P91,S8,PP4,PG1001

"Words are irrelevant to prayer; ... God answers the souls attitude, not the words." P91,S8,PP12,PG1002

"...prayer is not a process of getting your way but rather a program of taking God's way, an experience of learning how to recognize and execute the Father's will..." P180,S2,PP3,PG1946

"True religious worship is not a futile monologue of self-deception. Worship is a personal communion with that which is divinely real, with that which is the very source of reality. Man aspires by worship to be better and thereby eventually attains *the best.*" P196,S3,PP16,PG2095

CHAPTER 8: SELECTED TOPICS

This chapter contains my selection of favorite or interesting concepts and quotations. *The Urantia Book* contains much, much more, in better context, and more fully explained. Another person's interests may not match my own, but, this sampler of concepts and quotes should help in introducing the book.

a. *Cosmic Properties*

A concept of the immense size of inhabited creation, and the much greater size of the uninhabited four outer space levels, is presented in Chapter 3. The spiritual and time-space transcending attributes of the Isle of Paradise, which is the gravitational center of all creation, are also briefly portrayed, and summarized on the diagrams in that chapter. The Isle of Paradise is also "...the source and center of physical matter, and the absolute master pattern of universal material reality."
FOREWORD,SV,PP5,PG8

Creation contains spiritual as well as material realities, and includes personality, personal will, individual mind, and cosmic mind. Various attributes or properties of creation are portrayed in the following:

> "Solitary Messengers are, therefore, generally used for dispatch and service in those situations where personality is essential to the achievement of the assignment, and where it is desired to avoid the loss of time which would be occasioned by the sending of any other readily available type of personal messenger. They are the only definitely personalized beings who can synchronize with the combined universal currents of the grand universe. Their velocity in traversing space is variable, depending on a great variety of interfering influences, but the record shows that on the journey to fulfill this mission my associate messenger proceeded at the rate of 841,621,642,000 of your miles per second of your time." P23,S3,PP3,PG261

> "The four points of the compass are universal and inherent in the life of Nebadon. [Nebadon is the name of our local universe.] All living creatures possess bodily units which are sensitive and responsive to these directional currents. These creature creations are duplicated on down through the universe to the individual planets and, in conjunction with the magnetic forces of the worlds, so activate the hosts of microscopic bodies in the animal organism that these direction cells ever point north and south. Thus is the sense of orientation forever fixed in the living beings of the universe. This sense is not wholly wanting as a conscious possession by mankind. These bodies were first observed on Urantia about the time of this narration." P34,S4,PP11,PG378 [Circa 1935.]

> "I cannot, with exclusive spirit vision, perceive the building in which this narrative is being translated and recorded. A Divine Counselor from Uversa who chances to

stand by my side perceives still less of these purely material creations. We discern how these material structures appear to you by viewing a spirit counterpart presented to our minds by one of our attending energy transformers. This material building is not exactly real to me, a spirit being, but it is, of course, very real and very serviceable to material mortals." P44,PP9,PG498

"The finite universe of matter would eventually become uniform and deterministic but for the combined presence of mind and spirit. The influence of the cosmic mind constantly injects spontaneity into even the material worlds." P195,S6,PP15,PG2078

"... regarding the health-giving and disease-destroying properties of sunlight." P66,S5,PP20,PG748

"There are just three elements in universal reality: fact, idea, and relation. The religious consciousness identifies these realities as science, philosophy, and truth. Philosophy would be inclined to view these activities as reason, wisdom, and faith—physical reality, intellectual reality, and spiritual reality. We are in the habit of designating these realities as thing, meaning, and value." P196,S3,PP3,PG2094

b. *Matter and Energy; Undiscovered Energy*

The Urantia Book makes various references to realities not yet discovered here on Earth (as of about 1935.)

"Light, heat, electricity, magnetism, chemism, energy, and matter are—in origin, nature, and destiny—one and the same thing, together with other material realities as yet undiscovered on Urantia." P42,S4,PP1,PG472

"The mesotron explains certain cohesive properties of the atomic nucleus, but it does not account for the cohesion of proton to proton nor for the adhesion of neutron to neutron. The paradoxical and powerful force of atomic cohesive integrity is a form of energy as yet undiscovered on Urantia." P42,S8,PP6,PG479

"Matter—energy—for they are but diverse manifestations of the same cosmic reality, as a universe phenomenon is inherent in the Universal Father. "In him all things consist." Matter may appear to manifest inherent energy and to exhibit self-contained powers, but the lines of gravity involved in the energies concerned in all these physical phenomena are derived from, and are dependent on, Paradise. The ultimaton, the first measurable form of energy, has Paradise as its nucleus. P42,S1,PP2,PG467 [Ultimatons are also described as "... the basic units of materialized energy ..."] P42,S4,PP3,PG473

"There is innate in matter and present in universal space a form of energy not known on Urantia. When this discovery is finally made, then will physicists feel that they have solved, almost at least, the mystery of matter. And so will they have approached one step nearer the Creator; so will they have mastered one more phase of the divine technique; but in no sense will they have found God, neither will they have established the existence of matter or the operation of natural laws apart from the cosmic technique of Paradise and the motivating purpose of the Universal Father." P42,S1,PP3,PG467

"The savage is a slave to nature, but scientific civilization is slowly conferring increasing liberty on mankind. Through animals, fire, wind, water, electricity, and other undiscovered sources of energy, man has liberated, and will continue to liberate, himself from the necessity for unremitting toil. Regardless of the transient trouble produced by the prolific invention of machinery, the ultimate benefits to be derived from such mechanical inventions are inestimable. Civilization can never flourish, much less be established, until man has *leisure* to think, to plan, to imagine new and better ways of doing things." P81,S2,PP10,PG902

"The physical controllers are chiefly occupied in the adjustment of basic energies undiscovered on Urantia." P29,S4,PP7,PG325 [Physical controllers are a type of being.]

c. ***Suggestions for Living***

"The spirit world is governed on the principle of respecting your freewill choice provided the course you may choose is not detrimental to you or injurious to your fellows." P48,S6,PP4,PG552

"Having started out on the way of life everlasting, having accepted the assignment and received your orders to advance, do not fear the dangers of human forgetfulness and mortal inconstancy, do not be troubled with doubts of failure or by perplexing confusion, do not falter and question your status and standing, for in every dark hour, at every crossroad in the forward struggle, the Spirit of Truth will always speak, saying, "This is the way." P35,S7,PP8,PG383

"These are the mortals who have been commanded by the Universal Father, "Be you perfect, even as I am perfect." The Father has bestowed himself upon you, placed his own spirit within you; *therefore* does he demand ultimate perfection of you. The narrative of human ascent from the mortal spheres of time to the divine realms of eternity constitutes an intriguing recital not included in my assignment, but this supernal adventure should be the supreme study of mortal man." P40,S7,PP4,PG449

"Never, in all your ascent to Paradise, will you gain anything by impatiently attempting to circumvent the established and divine plan by short cuts, personal inventions, or other devices for improving on the way of perfection, to perfection, and for eternal perfection." P75,S8,PP5,PG846

The following are selected items concerning character taken from a list. The other items on the list are similar, and were deleted to keep this introduction shorter.

"1. A display of specialized skill does not signify possession of spiritual capacity. Cleverness is not a substitute for true character.

2. Few persons live up to the faith which they really have. Unreasoned fear is a master intellectual fraud practiced upon the evolving mortal soul.

3. Inherent capacities cannot be exceeded; a pint can never hold a quart. The spirit concept cannot be mechanically forced into the material memory mold.

4. Few mortals ever dare to draw anything like the sum of personality credits established by the combined ministries of nature and grace. The majority of impoverished souls are truly rich, but they refuse to believe it. ...

Chapter 8

11. The weak indulge in resolutions, but the strong act. Life is but a day's work—do it well. The act is ours; the consequences God's.

12. The greatest affliction of the cosmos is never to have been afflicted. Mortals only learn wisdom by experiencing tribulation. ...

19. Anxiety must be abandoned. The disappointments hardest to bear are those which never come. ...

22. The evolving soul is not made divine by what it does, but by what it strives to do. ...

28. The argumentative defense of any proposition is inversely proportional to the truth contained." P48,S7,PP3,PG556

The following are portions of a discourse on the art of living by Rodan of Alexander:

"1. *Mutual self-expression and self-understanding*. Many noble human impulses die because there is no one to hear their expression. Truly, it is not good for man to be alone. Some degree of recognition and a certain amount of appreciation are essential to the development of human character. Without the genuine love of a home, no child can achieve the full development of normal character. Character is something more than mere mind and morals. Of all social relations calculated to develop character, the most effective and ideal is the affectionate and understanding friendship of man and woman in the mutual embrace of intelligent wedlock. ...

2. *Union of souls - the mobilization of wisdom*. ... Fear, envy, and conceit can be prevented only by intimate contact with other minds. ...

3. *The enthusiasm for living*. Isolation tends to exhaust the energy charge of the soul. Association with one's fellows is essential to the renewal of the zest for life and is indispensable to the maintenance of the courage to fight those battles consequent upon the ascent to the higher levels of human living. Friendship enhances the joys and glorifies the triumphs of life. Loving and intimate human associations tend to rob suffering of its sorrow and hardship of much of its bitterness. The presence of a friend enhances all beauty and exalts every goodness. ...

4. *The enhanced defense against all evil*. Personality association and mutual affection is an efficient insurance against evil. Difficulties, sorrow, disappointment, and defeat are more painful and disheartening when borne alone. ... Man languishes in isolation. Human beings unfailingly become discouraged when they view only the transitory transactions of time. The present, when divorced from the past and the future, becomes exasperatingly trivial. Only a glimpse of the circle of eternity can inspire man to do his best and can challenge the best in him to do its utmost. And when man is thus at his best, he lives most unselfishly for the good of others, his fellow sojourners in time and eternity." P160,S2,PP6,PG1775

"Everything nonspiritual in human experience, excepting personality, is a means to an end. Every true relationship of mortal man with other persons—human or divine—is an end in itself. And such fellowship with the personality of Deity is the eternal goal of universe ascension." P112,S2,PP4,PG1228

"Let man enjoy himself; let the human race find pleasure in a thousand and one ways; let evolutionary mankind explore all forms of legitimate self- gratification, the fruits of the long upward biologic struggle. Man has well earned some of his present-day joys and pleasures. But look you well to the goal of destiny! Pleasures are indeed suicidal if they succeed in destroying property, which has become the institution of self-maintenance; and self-gratifications have indeed cost a fatal price if they bring about the collapse of marriage, the decadence of family life, and the destruction of the home—man's supreme evolutionary acquirement and civilization's only hope of survival." P84,S8,PP6,PG943

d. **More Historic Notes**

"Early evolutionary man is not a colorful creature. In general, these primitive mortals are cave dwellers or cliff residents. They also build crude huts in the large trees. Before they acquire a high order of intelligence, the planets are sometimes overrun with the larger types of animals. But early in this era mortals learn to kindle and maintain fire, and with the increase of inventive imagination and the improvement in tools, evolving man soon vanquishes the larger and more unwieldy animals. The early races also make extensive use of the larger flying animals. These enormous birds are able to carry one or two average-sized men for a nonstop flight of over five hundred miles. On some planets these birds are of great service since they possess a high order of intelligence, often being able to speak many words of the languages of the realm. These birds are most intelligent, very obedient, and unbelievably affectionate. Such passenger birds have been long extinct on Urantia, but your early ancestors enjoyed their services." P52,S1,PP5,PG590

"But Noah really lived; he was a wine maker of Aram, a river settlement near Erech. He kept a written record of the days of the river's rise from year to year. He brought much ridicule upon himself by going up and down the river valley advocating that all houses be built of wood, boat fashion, and that the family animals be put on board each night as the flood season approached. He would go to the neighboring river settlements every year and warn them that in so many days the floods would come. Finally a year came in which the annual floods were greatly augmented by unusually heavy rainfall so that the sudden rise of the waters wiped out the entire village; only Noah and his immediate family were saved in their houseboat." P78,S7,PP5,PG875

"Magic is natural to a savage. He believes that an enemy can actually be killed by practicing sorcery on his shingled hair or fingernail trimmings. The fatality of snake bites was attributed to the magic of the sorcerer. The difficulty in combating magic arises from the fact that fear can kill. Primitive peoples so feared magic that it did actually kill, and such results were sufficient to substantiate this erroneous belief. In case of failure there was always some plausible explanation; the cure for defective magic was more magic." P88,S4,PP6,PG971

"Today, men are not social slaves, but thousands allow ambition to enslave them to debt. Involuntary slavery has given way to a new and improved form of modified industrial servitude." P69,S8,PP10,PG780

e. *Equality, Race, Biologic Inheritance*

Race or biologic inheritance make no difference in a human's relationship with God. One's conscious or unconscious choices with respect to God's divine will are the meaningful criteria. Bodies are material vehicles; someone may be smarter, someone may run faster, but spiritually, people are equal.

> "One day while resting at lunch, about halfway to Tarentum, Ganid asked Jesus a direct question as to what he thought of India's caste system. Said Jesus: "Though human beings differ in many ways, the one from another, before God and in the spiritual world all mortals stand on an equal footing. There are only two groups of mortals in the eyes of God: those who desire to do his will and those who do not. As the universe looks upon an inhabited world, it likewise discerns two great classes: those who know God and those who do not. Those who cannot know God are reckoned among the animals of any given realm. Mankind can appropriately be divided into many classes in accordance with differing qualifications, as they may be viewed physically, mentally, socially, vocationally, or morally, but as these different classes of mortals appear before the judgment bar of God, they stand on an equal footing; God is truly no respecter of persons. Although you cannot escape the recognition of differential human abilities and endowments in matters intellectual, social, and moral, you should make no such distinctions in the spiritual brotherhood of men when assembled for worship in the presence of God." P133,PP3,PG1468

> "God is spirit, and God gives a fragment of his spirit self to dwell in the heart of man. Spiritually, all men are equal. The kingdom of heaven is free from castes, classes, social levels, and economic groups. You are all brethren." P134,S4,PP7,PG1487

As we shall see, *The Urantia Book* uses uncomplimentary words like inferior, defective, and subnormal in describing some biologic, and in some ways social, aspects of humanity. At the other end of the spectrum, it uses words like superior, higher types, and excellent specimens of humanity.

Our biologic uplifters, our Adam and Eve, defaulted. On a normal planet, the Adams and Eves not only bring superior biologic characteristics to the planet, but, along with the Planetary Prince and others, actually manage and improve the biologic characteristics of humanity. As a consequence of the default and the rebellion, generally speaking, our biologic stock could be better.

It is normal for colored races to appear on inhabited planets. An indication of the purpose of the colored races is given in the following:

> "The evolution of … [the races] … provides certain very desirable variations in mortal types and affords an otherwise unattainable expression of diverse human potentials. These modifications are beneficial to the progress of mankind as a whole provided they are subsequently upstepped by the imported Adamic or violet race." P51,S4,PP4,PG584 [We received a limited upstepping.]

According to *The Urantia Book* the races are not completely equal:

> "On worlds having all six evolutionary races the superior peoples are the first, third, and fifth races — the red, the yellow, and the blue. The evolutionary races thus alternate in capacity for intellectual growth and spiritual development, the second, fourth, and sixth being somewhat less endowed." P51,S4,PP3,PG584 [The second and fourth are the orange and green, who on earth are extinct or blended, and the sixth is indigo.]

This concept is likely to be controversial, considering the current state of race relations here on Earth. It is either true or not. I believe it to be true, because *The Urantia Book* rings true to me. If true, it will be true on the average; there are wide variations in all races. I have met persons I would call superior in all existing races. All humans are sons and daughters of God, all are spiritually equal, God is no respecter of persons, and relationship with the Creator (truth, beauty, goodness, love, service) is a true measure.

> "There are no pure races in the world today. The early and original evolutionary peoples of color have only two representative races persisting in the world, the yellow man and the black man; and even these two races are much admixed with the extinct colored peoples. While the so-called white race is predominantly descended from the ancient blue man, it is admixed more or less with all other races much as is the red man of the Americas." P82,S6,PP1,PG919

> "Hybridization of superior and dissimilar stocks is the secret of the creation of new and more vigorous strains. And this is true of plants, animals, and the human species. Hybridization augments vigor and increases fertility. Race mixtures of the average or superior strata of various peoples greatly increase creative potential, as is shown in the present population of the United States of North America. When such matings take place between the lower or inferior strata, creativity is diminished, as is shown by the present-day peoples of southern India." P82,S6,PP5,PG920

> "This problem of race improvement is not such an extensive undertaking when it is attacked at this early date in human evolution. The preceding period of tribal struggles and rugged competition in race survival has weeded out most of the abnormal and defective strains. An idiot does not have much chance of survival in a primitive and warring tribal social organization. It is the false sentiment of your partially perfected civilizations that fosters, protects, and perpetuates the hopelessly defective strains of evolutionary human stocks." P52,S2,PP11,PG592

> "From a world standpoint, overpopulation has never been a serious problem in the past, but if war is lessened and science increasingly controls human diseases, it may become a serious problem in the near future. At such a time the great test of the wisdom of world leadership will present itself. Will Urantia rulers have the insight and courage to foster the multiplication of the average or stabilized human being instead of the extremes of the supernormal and the enormously increasing groups of the subnormal? The normal man should be fostered; he is the backbone of civilization and the source of the mutant geniuses of the race. The subnormal man should be kept under society's control; no more should be produced than are required to administer the lower levels of industry, those tasks requiring intelligence above the animal level but making such low-grade demands as to prove veritable slavery and bondage for the higher types of mankind." P69,S6,PP11,PG770

f. *War*

Here are some Urantia Book viewpoints on war. It discusses warlike attributes of humanity, the past value of war in evolutionary development, and it presents criteria for achieving a true solution to the war problem.

"War is the natural state and heritage of evolving man; peace is the social yardstick measuring civilization's advancement. Before the partial socialization of the advancing races man was exceedingly individualistic, extremely suspicious, and unbelievably quarrelsome. Violence is the law of nature, hostility the automatic reaction of the children of nature, while war is but these same activities carried on collectively. And wherever and whenever the fabric of civilization becomes stressed by the complications of society's advancement, there is always an immediate and ruinous reversion to these early methods of violent adjustment of the irritations of human interassociations." P70,S1,PP1,PG783

"…Olden wars strengthened nations, but modern struggles disrupt civilized culture. Ancient warfare resulted in the decimation of inferior peoples; the net result of modern conflict is the selective destruction of the best human stocks. Early wars promoted organization and efficiency, but these have now become the aims of modern industry. During past ages war was a social ferment which pushed civilization forward; this result is now better attained by ambition and invention. Ancient warfare supported the concept of a God of battles, but modern man has been told that God is love. War has served many valuable purposes in the past, it has been an indispensable scaffolding in the building of civilization, but it is rapidly becoming culturally bankrupt--incapable of producing dividends of social gain in any way commensurate with the terrible losses attendant upon its invocation." P70,S2,PP4,PG786

"In past ages a fierce war would institute social changes and facilitate the adoption of new ideas such as would not have occurred naturally in ten thousand years. The terrible price paid for these certain war advantages was that society was temporarily thrown back into savagery; civilized reason had to abdicate. War is strong medicine, very costly and most dangerous; while often curative of certain social disorders, it sometimes kills the patient, destroys the society." P70,S2,PP1,PG785

"War has had a social value to past civilization because it:

1. Imposed discipline, enforced co-operation.

2. Put a premium on fortitude and courage.

3. Fostered and solidified nationalism.

4. Destroyed weak and unfit peoples.

5. Dissolved the illusion of primitive equality and selectively stratified society." P70,S2,PP3,PG785

"…Wise statesmen will sometime work for the welfare of humanity even while they strive to promote the interest of their national or racial groups. Selfish political sagacity is ultimately suicidal--destructive of all those enduring qualities which insure planetary group survival." P52,S6,PP6,PG598

"…The fact that the present-day peace groups have long since expanded beyond blood ties to embrace nations is most encouraging, despite the fact that Urantia nations are still spending vast sums on war preparations." P70,S4,PP1,PG788

"Ideas may take origin in the stimuli of the outer world, but ideals are born only in the creative realms of the inner world. Today the nations of the world are directed by men who have a superabundance of ideas, but they are poverty-stricken in ideals. That is the explanation of poverty, divorce, war, and racial hatreds." P111,S4,PP10,PG1220

"Do not make the mistake of glorifying war; rather discern what it has done for society so that you may the more accurately visualize what its substitutes must provide in order to continue the advancement of civilization. And if such adequate substitutes are not provided, then you may be sure that war will long continue." P70,S2,PP8,PG786

"Idealism can never survive on an evolving planet if the idealists in each generation permit themselves to be exterminated by the baser orders of humanity. And here is the great test of idealism: Can an advanced society maintain that military preparedness which renders it secure from all attack by its war-loving neighbors without yielding to the temptation to employ this military strength in offensive operations against other peoples for purposes of selfish gain or national aggrandizement? National survival demands preparedness, and religious idealism alone can prevent the prostitution of preparedness into aggression. Only love, brotherhood, can prevent the strong from oppressing the weak." P71,S4,PP5,PG804

The following quotes present criteria for peace on earth. Other criteria include the need for a global language, and the danger of changes in the social order that occur too quickly, resulting in instability.

"War on Urantia will never end so long as nations cling to the illusive notions of unlimited national sovereignty. There are only two levels of relative sovereignty on an inhabited world: the spiritual free will of the individual mortal and the collective sovereignty of mankind as a whole. Between the level of the individual human being and the level of the total of mankind, all groupings and associations are relative, transitory, and of value only in so far as they enhance the welfare, well-being, and progress of the individual and planetary grand total - man and mankind." P134,S5,PP2,PG1487

"Urantia will not enjoy lasting peace until the so-called sovereign nations intelligently and fully surrender their sovereign powers into the hands of the brotherhood of men--mankind government. Internationalism--Leagues of Nations--can never bring permanent peace to mankind. World-wide confederations of nations will effectively prevent minor wars and acceptably control the smaller nations, but they will not prevent world wars nor control the three, four, or five most powerful governments. In the face of real conflicts, one of these world powers will withdraw from the League and declare war. You cannot prevent nations going to war as long as they remain infected with the delusional virus of national sovereignty. Internationalism is a step in the right direction. An international police force will prevent many minor wars, but it will not be effective in preventing major wars, conflicts between the great military governments of earth." P134,S5,PP10,PG1489

"It is not a question of armaments or disarmament. Neither does the question of conscription or voluntary military service enter into these problems of maintaining world-wide peace. If you take every form of modern mechanical armaments and all types of explosives away from strong nations, they will fight with fists, stones, and clubs as long as they cling to their delusions of the divine right of national sovereignty." P134,S6,PP6, PG1490

"...Political sovereignty is innate with the peoples of the world. When all the peoples of Urantia create a world government, they have the right and the power to make such a government SOVEREIGN; and when such a representative or democratic world power controls the world's land, air, and naval forces, peace on earth and good will among men can prevail--but not until then.

To use an important nineteenth- and twentieth-century illustration: The forty-eight states of the American Federal Union have long enjoyed peace. They have no more wars among themselves. They have surrendered their sovereignty to the federal government, and through the arbitrament of war, they have abandoned all claims to the delusions of self-determination..." P134,S5,PP12,PG1489

"The bestowal Son is the Prince of Peace. He arrives with the message, "Peace on earth and good will among men." On normal worlds this is a dispensation of world-wide peace; the nations no more learn war. But such salutary influences did not attend the coming of your bestowal Son, Christ Michael. Urantia is not proceeding in the normal order. Your world is out of step in the planetary procession. Your Master, when on earth, warned his disciples that his advent would not bring the usual reign of peace on Urantia. He distinctly told them that there would be "wars and rumors of wars," and that nation would rise against nation. At another time he said, "Think not that I have come to bring peace upon earth." P52,S6,PP1,PG597

"With scientific progress, wars are going to become more and more devastating until they become almost racial suicidal. How many world wars must be fought and how may leagues of nations must fail before men will be willing to establish the government of mankind and begin to enjoy the blessings of permanent peace and thrive on the tranquility of good will - world-wide good will - among men?" P134,S6,PP17,PG1490

g. *Government, Civilization*

As we can see from the following two quotes, *The Urantia Book* presents attributes of good government. How do we get there? I think ethical progress is necessary. The revelations of the nature of the Creator and creation contained in *The Urantia Book* should help greatly in the long term. Establishing wise, humanity-serving government is a process, in which clarity of purpose and vision are of much benefit.

"There are ten steps, or stages, to the evolution of a practical and efficient form of representative government, and these are:

1. *Freedom of the person.* Slavery, serfdom, and all forms of human bondage must disappear.

2. *Freedom of the mind.* Unless a free people are educated—taught to think intelligently and plan wisely—freedom usually does more harm than good.

3. *The reign of law.* Liberty can be enjoyed only when the will and whims of human rulers are replaced by legislative enactments in accordance with accepted fundamental law.

4. *Freedom of speech.* Representative government is unthinkable without freedom of all forms of expression for human aspirations and opinions.

5. *Security of property.* No government can long endure if it fails to provide for the right to enjoy personal property in some form. Man craves the right to use, control, bestow, sell, lease, and bequeath his personal property.

6. *The right of petition.* Representative government assumes the right of citizens to be heard. The privilege of petition is inherent in free citizenship.

7. *The right to rule.* It is not enough to be heard; the power of petition must progress to the actual management of the government.

8. *Universal suffrage.* Representative government presupposes an intelligent, efficient, and universal electorate. The character of such a government will ever be determined by the character and caliber of those who compose it. As civilization progresses, suffrage, while remaining universal for both sexes, will be effectively modified, regrouped, and otherwise differentiated.

9. *Control of public servants.* No civil government will be serviceable and effective unless the citizenry possess and use wise techniques of guiding and controlling officeholders and public servants.

10. *Intelligent and trained representation.* The survival of democracy is dependent on successful representative government; and that is conditioned upon the practice of electing to public offices only those individuals who are technically trained, intellectually competent, socially loyal, and morally fit. Only by such provisions can government of the people, by the people, and for the people be preserved." P71,S2,PP4,PG802

"If men would maintain their freedom, they must, after having chosen their charter of liberty, provide for its wise, intelligent, and fearless interpretation to the end that there may be prevented:

1. Usurpation of unwarranted power by either the executive or legislative branches.
2. Machinations of ignorant and superstitious agitators.
3. Retardation of scientific progress.
4. Stalemate of the dominance of mediocrity.
5. Domination by vicious minorities.
6. Control by ambitious and clever would-be dictators.
7. Disastrous disruption of panics.
8. Exploitation by the unscrupulous.
9. Taxation enslavement of the citizenry by the state.
10. Failure of social and economic fairness.
11. Union of church and state.
12. Loss of personal liberty." P70,S12,PP6,PG798

"No civilization can survive the long-time harboring of large classes of unemployed. In time, even the best of citizens will become distorted and demoralized by accepting support from the public treasury. Even private charity becomes pernicious when long extended to able-bodied citizens." P81,S6,PP32,PG910

The Urantia Book includes a paper portraying government on a neighboring planet. This provides an interesting and educational contrast to our own forms of government. I have included excerpts in the next chapter.

h. Nature

"Nature is in a limited sense the physical habit of God." P4,S2,PP1,PG56

"Perfection is in nature, but nature is not perfect." P9,S5,PP5,PG103

"Nature confers no rights on man, only life and a world in which to live it. Nature does not even confer the right to live, as might be deduced by considering what would likely happen if an unarmed man met a hungry tiger face to face in the primitive forest. Society's prime gift to man is security." P70,S9,PP1,PG793

"Nature is a time-space resultant of two cosmic factors: first, the immutability, perfection, and rectitude of Paradise Deity, and second, the experimental plans, executive blunders, insurrectionary errors, incompleteness of development, and imperfection of wisdom of the extra-Paradise creatures, from the highest to the lowest. Nature therefore carries a uniform, unchanging, majestic, and marvelous thread of perfection from the circle of eternity; but in each universe, on each planet, and in each individual life, this nature is modified, qualified, and perchance marred by the acts, the mistakes, and the disloyalties of the creatures of the evolutionary systems and universes; and therefore must nature ever be of a changing mood, whimsical withal, though stable underneath, and varied in accordance with the operating procedures of a local universe." P4,S2,PP3,PG56

"And nature is marred, her beautiful face is scarred, her features are seared, by the rebellion, the misconduct, the misthinking of the myriads of creatures who are a part of nature, but who have contributed to her disfigurement in time. No, nature is not God. Nature is not an object of worship." P4,S2,PP8,PG57

i. Spirit and Flesh

The Urantia Book discusses conflicts that can arise between our animal heritage and tendencies, and our nature-transcending spiritual powers. The first quote points out that we can have both, and the two following quotes portray these conflicts.

"The normal urges of animal beings and the natural appetites and impulses of the physical nature are not in conflict with even the highest spiritual attainment except in the minds of ignorant, mistaught, or unfortunately overconscientious persons." P34,S7,PP7,PG383

"In every mortal there exists a dual nature: the inheritance of animal tendencies and the high urge of spirit endowment. During the short life you live on Urantia, these two diverse and opposing urges can seldom be fully reconciled; they can hardly be harmonized and unified; but throughout your lifetime the combined spirit ever ministers to assist you in subjecting the flesh more and more to the leading of the spirit. Even though you must live your material life through, even though you cannot escape the body and its necessities, nonetheless, in purpose and ideals you are empowered increasingly to subject the animal nature to the mastery of the spirit. There truly exists within you a conspiracy of spiritual forces, a confederation of divine powers, whose exclusive purpose is to effect your final deliverance from material bondage and finite handicaps." P34,S6,PP9,PG381

"It is only natural that mortal man should be harassed by feelings of insecurity as he views himself inextricably bound to nature while he possesses spiritual powers wholly transcendent to all things temporal and finite. Only religious confidence—living faith—can sustain man amid such difficult and perplexing problems." P111,S6,PP8,PG1222

j. ***Finding Eden***

I wonder if remnants of the Garden of Eden (the first garden) might be found. It existed about 38,000 years ago, had many paved roads and brick structures, and at least one stone structure. It was submerged by geologic processes about 34,000 years ago, so it may be covered by sediments, or have decayed (the bricks may have lost their cementation) since that time. However, remnants of stone structures should remain. The Garden of Eden was the home of our Adam and Eve, until they defaulted. The following quotes provide concepts of the garden, which was real. It was located on "… a long narrow peninsula — almost an island—projecting westward from the eastern shores of the Mediterranean Sea." P73,S3,PP1,PG823

"The first task was the building of the brick wall across the neck of the peninsula. This once completed, the real work of landscape beautification and home building could proceed unhindered.

A zoological garden was created by building a smaller wall just outside the main wall; the intervening space, occupied by all manner of wild beasts, served as an additional defense against hostile attacks. This menagerie was organized in twelve grand divisions, and walled paths led between these groups to the twelve gates of the Garden, the river and its adjacent pastures occupying the central area." P73,S4,PP2,PG824

"At the center of the Edenic peninsula was the exquisite stone temple of the Universal Father, the sacred shrine of the Garden. To the north the administrative headquarters was established; to the south were built the homes for the workers and their families; to the west was provided the allotment of ground for the proposed schools of the educational system of the expected Son, while in the "east of Eden" were built the domiciles intended for the promised Son and his immediate offspring. The architectural plans for Eden provided homes and abundant land for one million human beings.

At the time of Adam's arrival, though the Garden was only one-fourth finished, it had thousands of miles of irrigation ditches and more than twelve thousand miles of paved paths and roads. There were a trifle over five thousand brick buildings in the various sectors, and the trees and plants were almost beyond number. Seven was the largest number of houses composing any one cluster in the park. And though the structures of the Garden were simple, they were most artistic. The roads and paths were well built, and the landscaping was exquisite." P73,S5,PP1,PG824

"Before the disruption of the Adamic regime a covered brick-conduit disposal system had been constructed which ran beneath the walls and emptied into the river of Eden almost a mile beyond the outer or lesser wall of the Garden." P73,S5,PP4,PG825

"The peninsula had been overrun by these lower-grade Nodites for almost four thousand years after Adam left the Garden when, in connection with the violent activity of the surrounding volcanoes and the submergence of the Sicilian land bridge to Africa, the eastern floor of the Mediterranean Sea sank, carrying down beneath the waters the whole of the Edenic peninsula. Concomitant with this vast submergence the coast line of the eastern Mediterranean was greatly elevated. And this was the end of the most beautiful natural creation that Urantia has ever harbored. The sinking was not sudden, several hundred years being required completely to submerge the entire peninsula."
P73,S7,PP1,PG826

k. *Food for Thought*

There are many concepts presented in *The Urantia Book* that are difficult, at least for me, to understand. Part of the cause is that the revelators were constrained to work within our language, while they endeavored to portray various attributes of God and universe reality with which we are unfamiliar.

I have included the following to demonstrate part of this depth and complexity. Such teachings tend to become more comprehensible when studied over time and in context. The following are not in context; they are examples. There are aspects of God and universe reality that transcend time, space, and matter. But from these quotes you might surmise that not all of *The Urantia Book* is easy reading about easy concepts.

"Always remember: Potential infinity is absolute and inseparable from eternity. Actual infinity in time can never be anything but partial and must therefore be nonabsolute; neither can infinity of actual personality be absolute except in unqualified Deity. And it is the differential of infinity potential in the Unqualified Absolute and the Deity Absolute that eternalizes the Universal Absolute, thereby making it cosmically possible to have material universes in space and spiritually possible to have finite personalities in time.

The finite can coexist in the cosmos along with the Infinite only because the associative presence of the Universal Absolute so perfectly equalizes the tensions between time and eternity, finity and infinity, reality potential and reality actuality, Paradise and space, man and God. Associatively the Universal Absolute constitutes the identification of the zone of progressing evolutional reality existent in the time-space, and in the transcended time-space, universes of subinfinite Deity manifestation."
FOREWORD,SXI,PP12,PG15

"On first thought, a concept of the Absolute as ancestor to all things—even the Trinity—seems to afford transitory satisfaction of consistency gratification and philosophic unification, but any such conclusion is invalidated by the actuality of the eternity of the Paradise Trinity. We are taught, and we believe, that the Universal Father and his Trinity associates are eternal in nature and existence. There is, then, but one consistent philosophic conclusion, and that is: The Absolute is, to all universe intelligences, the impersonal and co-ordinate reaction of the Trinity (of Trinities) to all basic and primary space situations, intrauniversal and extrauniversal. To all personality intelligences of the grand universe the Paradise Trinity forever stands in finality, eternity, supremacy, and ultimacy and, for all practical purposes of personal comprehension and creature realization, as absolute." P56,S9,PP4,PG644

CHAPTER 9: GOVERNMENT ON A NEIGHBORING PLANET

The Urantia Book has a paper discussing government of a nation on neighboring planet. I have included excerpts, because the national culture portrayed has positive values that we might learn from. They have evolved into a nation that is active in bettering life for its citizens, and it is this attitude that I find refreshing.

First, it is unusual for us to have received this information:

> "Of all the Satania [our local system] worlds which became isolated because of participation in the Lucifer rebellion, this planet has experienced a history most like that of Urantia. The similarity of the two spheres undoubtedly explains why permission to make this extraordinary presentation was granted, for it is most unusual for the system rulers to consent to the narration on one planet of the affairs of another." P72,PP2,PG808

The purpose of presenting this material to us is explained as follows:

> "This recital of the affairs of a neighboring planet is made by special permission with the intent of advancing civilization and augmenting governmental evolution on Urantia. Much more could be narrated that would no doubt interest and intrigue Urantians, but this disclosure covers the limits of our permissive mandate." P72,S12,PP3,PG820

This paper in *The Urantia Book* is in 12 sections, each covering a different topic. The 12 section titles give an idea of the scope of this paper, so I am including them. Quoted excerpts from each section are presented beneath the appropriate section title.

a. *The Continental Nation*

> "These people are self-sustaining, that is, they can live indefinitely without importing anything from the surrounding nations. Their natural resources are replete, and by scientific techniques they have learned how to compensate for their deficiencies in the essentials of life. They enjoy a brisk domestic commerce but have little foreign trade owing to the universal hostility of their less progressive neighbors.
>
> This continental nation, in general, followed the evolutionary trend of the planet: The development from the tribal stage to the appearance of strong rulers and kings occupied thousands of years. The unconditional monarchs were succeeded by many different orders of government—abortive republics, communal states, and dictators came and went in endless profusion." P72,S1,PP3,PG808

Chapter 9

Then,

"The unified state progressed under strong monarchial rule for over one hundred years, during which there evolved a masterful charter of liberty.

The subsequent transition from monarchy to a representative form of government was gradual, the kings remaining as mere social or sentimental figureheads, finally disappearing when the male line of descent ran out. The present republic has now been in existence just two hundred years, during which time there has been a continuous progression toward the governmental techniques about to be narrated, the last developments in industrial and political realms having been made within the past decade." P72,S1,PP4,PG809

b. Political Organization

"There are five different types of metropolitan government, depending on the size of the city, but no city is permitted to have more than one million inhabitants. On the whole, these municipal governing schemes are very simple, direct, and economical. The few offices of city administration are keenly sought by the highest types of citizens." P72,S2,PP2,PG809

"The socioeconomic courts function in the following three divisions:

1. *Parental courts*, associated with the legislative and executive divisions of the home and social system.
2. *Educational courts*—the juridical bodies connected with the state and regional school systems and associated with the executive and legislative branches of the educational administrative mechanism.
3. *Industrial courts*—the jurisdictional tribunals vested with full authority for the settlement of all economic misunderstandings." P72,S2,PP7,PG810

c. The Home Life

"On this continent it is against the law for two families to live under the same roof. And since group dwellings have been outlawed, most of the tenement type of buildings have been demolished. But the unmarried still live in clubs, hotels, and other group dwellings. The smallest homesite permitted must provide fifty thousand square feet of land. All land and other property used for home purposes are free from taxation up to ten times the minimum homesite allotment.

The home life of this people has greatly improved during the last century. Attendance of parents, both fathers and mothers, at the parental schools of child culture is compulsory. Even the agriculturists who reside in small country settlements carry on this work by correspondence, going to the near-by centers for oral instruction once in ten days—every two weeks, for they maintain a five-day week.

The average number of children in each family is five, and they are under the full control of their parents or, in case of the demise of one or both, under that of the guardians designated by the parental courts. It is considered a great honor for any family to be awarded the guardianship of a full orphan. Competitive examinations are held among parents, and the orphan is awarded to the home of those displaying the best parental qualifications.

These people regard the home as the basic institution of their civilization. It is expected that the most valuable part of a child's education and character training will be secured from his parents and at home, and fathers devote almost as much attention to child culture as do mothers.

All sex instruction is administered in the home by parents or by legal guardians. Moral instruction is offered by teachers during the rest periods in the school shops, but not so with religious training, which is deemed to be the exclusive privilege of parents, religion being looked upon as an integral part of home life." P72,S3,PP1,PG811

d. *The Educational System*

"The educational system of this nation is compulsory and coeducational in the precollege schools that the student attends from the ages of five to eighteen. These schools are vastly different from those of Urantia. There are no classrooms, only one study is pursued at a time, and after the first three years all pupils become assistant teachers, instructing those below them. Books are used only to secure information that will assist in solving the problems arising in the school shops and on the school farms. Much of the furniture used on the continent and the many mechanical contrivances—this is a great age of invention and mechanization—are produced in these shops. Adjacent to each shop is a working library where the student may consult the necessary reference books. Agriculture and horticulture are also taught throughout the entire educational period on the extensive farms adjoining every local school." P72,S4,PP1,PG812

"Everyone takes one month's vacation each year. The precollege schools are conducted for nine months out of the year of ten, the vacation being spent with parents or friends in travel. This travel is a part of the adult-education program and is continued throughout a lifetime, the funds for meeting such expenses being accumulated by the same methods as those employed in old-age insurance." P72,S4,PP3,PG812

e. *Industrial Organization*

"The industrial situation among this people is far from their ideals; capital and labor still have their troubles, but both are becoming adjusted to the plan of sincere co-operation. On this unique continent the workers are increasingly becoming shareholders in all industrial concerns; every intelligent laborer is slowly becoming a small capitalist.

Social antagonisms are lessening, and good will is growing apace." P72,S5,PP1,PG813

"Every ten years the regional executives adjust and decree the lawful hours of daily gainful toil. Industry now operates on a five-day week, working four and playing one. These people labor six hours each working day and, like students, nine months in the year of ten. Vacation is usually spent in travel, and new methods of transportation having been so recently developed, the whole nation is travel bent. The climate favors travel about eight months in the year, and they are making the most of their opportunities.

Two hundred years ago the profit motive was wholly dominant in industry, but today it is being rapidly displaced by other and higher driving forces. Competition is keen on this continent, but much of it has been transferred from industry to play, skill, scientific achievement, and intellectual attainment. It is most active in social service and governmental loyalty. Among this people public service is rapidly becoming the chief goal of ambition. The richest man on the continent works six hours a day in the office of his machine shop and then hastens over to the local branch of the school of statesmanship, where he seeks to qualify for public service." P72,S5,PP6,PG813

"These people are also beginning to foster a new form of social disgust—disgust for both idleness and unearned wealth. Slowly but certainly they are conquering their machines. Once they, too, struggled for political liberty and subsequently for economic freedom. Now are they entering upon the enjoyment of both while in addition they are beginning to appreciate their well-earned leisure, which can be devoted to increased self-realization." P72,S5,PP9,PG814

f. **Old-age Insurance**

"This nation is making a determined effort to replace the self-respect-destroying type of charity by dignified government-insurance guarantees of security in old age. This nation provides every child an education and every man a job; therefore can it successfully carry out such an insurance scheme for the protection of the infirm and aged." P72,S6,PP1,PG814

"The funds for old-age pensions are derived from four sources:

1. One day's earnings each month are requisitioned by the federal government for this purpose, and in this country everybody works.
2. Bequests—many wealthy citizens leave funds for this purpose.
3. The earnings of compulsory labor in the state mines. After the conscript workers support themselves and set aside their own retirement contributions, all excess profits on their labor are turned over to this pension fund.
4. The income from natural resources. All natural wealth on the continent is held as a social trust by the federal government, and the income therefrom is utilized for social purposes, such as disease prevention, education of geniuses, and expenses of especially promising individuals in the statesmanship schools. One half of the income from natural resources goes to the old-age pension fund." P72,S6,PP3,PG814

"These government funds have long been honestly administered. Next to treason and murder, the heaviest penalties meted out by the courts are attached to betrayal of public trust. Social and political disloyalty are now looked upon as being the most heinous of all crimes." P72,S6,PP5,PG814

g. **Taxation**

"The federal government is paternalistic only in the administration of old-age pensions and in the fostering of genius and creative originality; the state governments are slightly more concerned with the individual citizen, while the local governments are much more paternalistic or socialistic. The city (or some subdivision thereof) concerns itself with such matters as health, sanitation, building regulations, beautification, water supply, lighting, heating, recreation, music, and communication." P72,S7,PP1,PG815

"Income to support the federal government is derived from the following five sources:

1. *Import duties.* All imports are subject to a tariff designed to protect the standard of living on this continent, which is far above that of any other nation on the planet. These tariffs are set by the highest industrial court after both houses of the industrial congress have ratified the recommendations of the chief executive of economic affairs, who is the joint appointee of these two legislative bodies. The upper industrial house is elected by labor, the lower by capital.

2. *Royalties.* The federal government encourages invention and original creations in the ten regional laboratories, assisting all types of geniuses—artists, authors, and scientists—and protecting their patents. In return the government takes one half the profits realized from all such inventions and creations, whether pertaining to machines, books, artistry, plants, or animals.

3. *Inheritance tax.* The federal government levies a graduated inheritance tax ranging from one to fifty per cent, depending on the size of an estate as well as on other conditions.

4. *Military equipment.* The government earns a considerable sum from the leasing of military and naval equipment for commercial and recreational usages.

5. *Natural resources.* The income from natural resources, when not fully required for the specific purposes designated in the charter of federal statehood, is turned into the national treasury." P72,S7,PP8,PG813

h. The Special Colleges

In addition to its basic education system, this nation has special schools for statesmanship, philosophy, science, professional training, and military/naval.

i. The Plan of Universal Suffrage

"2. Upon nomination by the state governors or by the regional executives and by the mandate of the regional supreme councils, individuals who have rendered great service to society, or who have demonstrated extraordinary wisdom in government service, may have additional votes conferred upon them not oftener than every five years and not to exceed nine such superfranchises. The maximum suffrage of any multiple voter is ten. Scientists, inventors, teachers, philosophers, and spiritual leaders are also thus recognized and honored with augmented political power. These advanced civic privileges are conferred by the state and regional supreme councils much as degrees are bestowed by the special colleges, and the recipients are proud to attach the symbols of such civic recognition, along with their other degrees, to their lists of personal achievements." P72,S9,PP3,PG817

"The schools of statesmanship have power to start proceedings in the state courts looking toward the disenfranchisement of any defective, idle, indifferent, or criminal individual. These people recognize that, when fifty per cent of a nation is inferior or defective and possesses the ballot, such a nation is doomed. They believe the dominance of mediocrity spells the downfall of any nation. Voting is compulsory, heavy fines being assessed against all who fail to cast their ballots." P72,S9,PP8,PG818

j. Dealing With Crime

"The methods of this people in dealing with crime, insanity, and degeneracy, while in some ways pleasing, will, no doubt, in others prove shocking to most Urantians.

Ordinary criminals and the defectives are placed, by sexes, in different agricultural colonies and are more than self-supporting. The more serious habitual criminals and the incurably insane are sentenced to death in the lethal gas chambers by the courts. Numerous crimes aside from murder, including betrayal of governmental trust, also carry the death penalty, and the visitation of justice is sure and swift." P72,S10,PP1,PG818

k. *Military Preparedness*

"Although these people maintain a powerful war establishment as a defense against invasion by the surrounding hostile peoples, it may be recorded to their credit that they have not in over one hundred years employed these military resources in an offensive war. They have become civilized to that point where they can vigorously defend civilization without yielding to the temptation to utilize their war powers in aggression. There have been no civil wars since the establishment of the united continental state, but during the last two centuries these people have been called upon to wage nine fierce defensive conflicts, three of which were against mighty confederations of world powers. Although this nation maintains adequate defense against attack by hostile neighbors, it pays far more attention to the training of statesmen, scientists, and philosophers.

When at peace with the world, all mobile defense mechanisms are quite fully employed in trade, commerce, and recreation. When war is declared, the entire nation is mobilized. Throughout the period of hostilities military pay obtains in all industries, and the chiefs of all military departments become members of the chief executive's cabinet." P72,S11,PP4,PG819

l. *The Other Nations*

"Although the society and government of this unique people are in many respects superior to those of the Urantia nations, it should be stated that on the other continents (there are eleven on this planet) the governments are decidedly inferior to the more advanced nations of Urantia.

Just now this superior government is planning to establish ambassadorial relations with the inferior peoples, and for the first time a great religious leader has arisen who advocates the sending of missionaries to these surrounding nations. We fear they are about to make the mistake that so many others have made when they have endeavored to force a superior culture and religion upon other races. What a wonderful thing could be done on this world if this continental nation of advanced culture would only go out and bring to itself the best of the neighboring peoples and then, after educating them, send them back as emissaries of culture to their benighted brethren! Of course, if a Magisterial Son should soon come to this advanced nation, great things could quickly happen on this world." P72,S12,PP1,PG819

CHAPTER 10: SPIRITUAL MINISTRIES TO HUMANS

Your personality is a gift of God, and, you are a sovereign will creature. You are free to choose.

"Personality is never spontaneous; it is the gift of the Paradise Father." FORWORD,SV,PP4,PG8

"The Universal Father never imposes any form of arbitrary recognition, formal worship, or slavish service upon the intelligent will creatures of the universes. The evolutionary inhabitants of the worlds of time and space must of themselves—in their own hearts—recognize, love, and voluntarily worship him. The Creator refuses to coerce or compel the submission of the spiritual free wills of his material creatures. The affectionate dedication of the human will to the doing of the Father's will is man's choicest gift to God; in fact, such a consecration of creature will constitutes man's only possible gift of true value to the Paradise Father. In God, man lives, moves, and has his being; there is nothing which man can give to God except this choosing to abide by the Father's will, and such decisions, effected by the intelligent will creatures of the universes, constitute the reality of that true worship which is so satisfying to the love-dominated nature of the Creator Father." P1,S1,PP2,PG22

There are ministries provided to help you choose, to help you find and grow toward God. The various ministries come from various attributes of God, and these are unified, co-ordinated.

Various ministries to humans include:

- The indwelling fragment of God, the Thought Adjuster or Mystery Monitor (an actual fragment of the Paradise Father, within you)
- The Holy Spirit, the Spirit of the local universe Divine Minister or Mother Spirit, who is a representative of the Paradise Infinite Spirit
- The seven adjutant mind-spirits bestowed by the local universe Divine Minister
- Our local universe Creator Son (Christ), and the Creator Son's bestowed Spirit of Truth.
- Seraphic ministries (angels)
- Co-ordinated ministry
- Midwayers, who are planetary inhabitants that serve the cause of goodness here on Earth. Midwayers are midway between mortals and angels.

The Paradise Eternal Son and the Paradise Infinite Spirit downstep themselves, you might say, all the way down to be available to the lowest orders of will creatures, humans. The Paradise Father doesn't thus downstep himself, but maintains personal contact with each individual through the presence of the indwelling fragment of himself, the Adjuster.

a. *The Indwelling Fragment of God, the Thought Adjuster or Mystery Monitor*

At the time of a person's first moral choice, currently at about age 5 years and 10 months on the average, the Heavenly Creator gives a fragment of himself to indwell that person's mind, and this is currently true for every normal minded human on the planet. This indwelling fragment of God, called the "Thought Adjuster" or "Mystery Monitor", continually works with you to lead you Godward. You might say that from about age 5, God has been with you, superconsciously perhaps, letting you know the divine will.

"The divine spirit arrives simultaneously with the first moral activity of the human mind, and that is the occasion of the birth of the soul." P133,S6,PP5,PG1478

"Thus they begin work with a definite and predetermined plan for the intellectual and spiritual development of their human subjects, but it is not incumbent upon any human being to accept this plan. You are all subjects of predestination, but it is not foreordained that you must accept this divine predestination; you are at full liberty to reject any part or all of the Thought Adjusters' program. ... The Adjusters respect your sovereignty of personality; *they are always subservient to your will.*" P110,S2,PP1,PG1204

"I wish it were possible for me to help evolving mortals to achieve a better understanding and attain a fuller appreciation of the unselfish and superb work of the Adjusters living within them, who are so devoutly faithful to the task of fostering man's spiritual welfare. ... I wish you could love them more, co-operate with them more fully, and cherish them more affectionately.

Although the divine indwellers are chiefly concerned with your spiritual preparation for the next stage of the never-ending existence, they are also deeply interested in your temporal welfare and in your real achievements on earth. They are delighted to contribute to your health, happiness, and true prosperity. They are not indifferent to your success in all matters of planetary advancement which are not inimical to your future life of eternal progress." P110,S1,PP2,PG1203

"The Adjuster remains with you in all disaster and through every sickness which does not wholly destroy the mentality. But how unkind knowingly to defile or otherwise deliberately to pollute the physical body, which must serve as the earthly tabernacle of this marvelous gift from God. All physical poisons greatly retard the efforts of the Adjuster to exalt the material mind, while the mental poisons of fear, anger, envy, jealousy, suspicion, and intolerance likewise tremendously interfere with the spiritual progress of the evolving soul." P110,S1,PP5,PG1204

"It is the indwelling Adjuster who individualizes the love of God to each human soul." P2,S5,PP10,PG40 [Your author likes this; to me it means that God works with each of us individually, within our own framework.]

"The infinity of the perfection of God is such that it eternally constitutes him mystery. ... the divine presence in the mind of man is the mystery of mysteries." P1,S4,PP1,PG26

b. *The Holy Spirit of the Local Universe Divine Minister or Mother Spirit*

The local universe Mother Spirit, who is a daughter of the Paradise Infinite Spirit, has her own ministering Spirit, the Holy Spirit.

> "In your sacred writings the term *Spirit of God* seems to be used interchangeably to designate both the Infinite Spirit on Paradise and the Creative Spirit of your local universe. The Holy Spirit is the spiritual circuit of this Creative Daughter of the Paradise Infinite Spirit. The Holy Spirit is a circuit indigenous to each local universe and is confined to the spiritual realm of that creation; but the Infinite Spirit is omnipresent." P8,S5,PP3,PG95

> "The presence of the universal spirit of the Eternal Son we *know*—we can unmistakably recognize it. The presence of the Infinite Spirit the Third Person of Deity, even mortal man may know, for material creatures can actually experience the beneficence of this divine influence which functions as the Holy Spirit of local universe bestowal upon the races of mankind. Human beings can also in some degree become conscious of the Adjuster, the impersonal presence of the Universal Father. These divine spirits which work for man's uplifting and spiritualization all act in unison and in perfect co-operation. They are as one in the spiritual operation of the plans of mortal ascension and perfection attainment." P9,S2,PP5,PG100

c. *The Seven Adjutant Mind-spirits Bestowed by the Local Universe Divine Minister or Mother Spirit*

The seven adjutant mind spirits are basic to all mental life on the planet, animal and human. They are non-personal, except that they originate with the local universe Divine Minister. They are more like circuits than entities. Humans share the first five of the adjutant mind-spirits with animals, and these are the spirits of intuition, understanding, courage, knowledge, and council. Animals do not have the spirit of worship and the spirit of wisdom. Otherwise, humans are animals.

> "It is the presence of the seven adjutant mind-spirits on the primitive worlds that conditions the course of organic evolution; that explains why evolution is purposeful and not accidental. These adjutants represent that function of the mind ministry of the Infinite Spirit which is extended to the lower orders of intelligent life through the operations of a local universe Mother Spirit. The adjutants are the children of the Universe Mother Spirit and constitute her personal ministry to the material minds of the realms. Wherever and whenever such mind is manifest, these spirits are variously functioning." P36,S5,PP1,PG401

> "... We are handicapped for words adequately to designate these seven adjutant mind-spirits. They are ministers of the lower levels of experiential mind, and they may be described, in the order of evolutionary attainment, as follows:
>
> 1. *The spirit of intuition*—quick perception, the primitive physical and inherent reflex instincts, the directional and other self-preservative endowments of all mind creations; the only one of the adjutants to function so largely in the lower orders of animal life and the only one to make extensive functional contact with the nonteachable levels of mechanical mind.

2. The spirit of understanding—the impulse of co-ordination, the spontaneous and apparently automatic association of ideas. This is the gift of the co-ordination of acquired knowledge, the phenomenon of quick reasoning, rapid judgment, and prompt decision.

3. The spirit of courage—the fidelity endowment—in personal beings, the basis of character acquirement and the intellectual root of moral stamina and spiritual bravery. When enlightened by facts and inspired by truth, this becomes the secret of the urge of evolutionary ascension by the channels of intelligent and conscientious self-direction.

4. The spirit of knowledge—the curiosity-mother of adventure and discovery, the scientific spirit; the guide and faithful associate of the spirits of courage and counsel; the urge to direct the endowments of courage into useful and progressive paths of growth.

5. The spirit of counsel—the social urge, the endowment of species co-operation; the ability of will creatures to harmonize with their fellows; the origin of the gregarious instinct among the more lowly creatures.

6. The spirit of worship—the religious impulse, the first differential urge separating mind creatures into the two basic classes of mortal existence. The spirit of worship forever distinguishes the animal of its association from the soulless creatures of mind endowment. Worship is the badge of spiritual-ascension candidacy.

7. The spirit of wisdom—the inherent tendency of all moral creatures towards orderly and progressive evolutionary advancement. This is the highest of the adjutants, the spirit co-ordinator and articulator of the work of all the others. This spirit is the secret of that inborn urge of mind creatures which initiates and maintains the practical and effective program of the ascending scale of existence; that gift of living things which accounts for their inexplicable ability to survive and, in survival, to utilize the co-ordination of all their past experience and present opportunities for the acquisition of all of everything that all of the other six mental ministers can mobilize in the mind of the organism concerned. Wisdom is the acme of intellectual performance. Wisdom is the goal of a purely mental and moral existence.P36,S5,PP5,PG402

"... the function of the first five in the animal orders is to a certain extent essential to the function of all seven as human intellect. This animal relationship makes the adjutants more practically effective as human mind; hence animals are to a certain extent indispensable to man's intellectual as well as to his physical evolution." P36,S5,PP13,PG403

d.   *Our Local Universe Creator Son and his Bestowed Spirit of Truth*

Another ministry is the Creator Son of our local universe, and his Spirit of Truth. As discussed more fully in a subsequent chapter, our planet, Urantia, is unique in that our local universe Creator Son walked this planet incarnated in human form, Jesus of Nazareth, God in man. This incarnation was a revelation and a bestowal, or gift, to this planet. You can personally get to know our local universe Creator Son, not only through his human life and how he lived it, but directly in your own personal experience. And part of this gift to our planet is his bestowed Spirit of Truth, which acts to let you know the truth of the Creator Son. The Spirit of Truth was poured out on all flesh at Pentecost.

"Remember that I have said: "Behold, I stand at the door and knock, and if any man will open, I will come in." P159,S3,PP2,PG1765

"Do not overlook the fact that the Spirit of Truth was bestowed upon all sincere believers; this gift of the spirit did not come only to the apostles. The one hundred and twenty men and women assembled in the upper chamber all received the new teacher, as did all the honest of heart throughout the whole world. This new teacher was bestowed upon mankind, and every soul received him in accordance with the love for truth and the capacity to grasp and comprehend spiritual realities. At last, true religion is delivered from the custody of priests and all sacred classes and finds its real manifestation in the individual souls of men." P194,S3,PP6,PG2063

"Pentecost was designed to lessen the self-assertiveness of individuals, groups, nations, and races. It is this spirit of self-assertiveness which so increases in tension that it periodically breaks loose in destructive wars. Mankind can be unified only by the spiritual approach, and the Spirit of Truth is a world influence which is universal." P194,S3,PP18,PG2065

"... the Spirit of Truth, who directs the loving contact of one human being with another." P180,S5,PP11,PG1950

"... Spirit of Truth ..., in every crisis of ascension unfailingly directing the Paradise pilgrim, ever saying: "This is the way...." P117,S5,PP9,PG1286

"And now that he has personally left the world, he sends in his place his Spirit of Truth, who is designed to live in man and, for each new generation, to restate the Jesus message so that every new group of mortals to appear upon the face of the earth shall have a new and up-to-date version of the gospel, just such personal enlightenment and group guidance as will prove to be an effective solvent for man's ever-new and varied spiritual difficulties.

The first mission of this spirit is, of course, to foster and personalize truth, for it is the comprehension of truth that constitutes the highest form of human liberty." P194,S2,PP1,PG2060

e. *Seraphic Ministries (Angels)*

There are many types and functions of angels throughout inhabited creation. There are incredible numbers of planetary, local universe, and superuniverse angels, hosts of them. They are the children or offspring of the Infinite Spirit. On the planetary level, for example, among an order called the Planetary Helpers, there are Quickeners of Morality, Spirits of Brotherhood, and Recorders. Angels act as guardians of destiny for humans. There are also Cherubim and Sanobim, who are "the faithful and efficient aids of the seraphic ministers, and all seven orders of seraphim are provided with these subordinate assistants." P38,S7,PP3,PG422

"Angels do not have material bodies, but they are definite and discrete beings; they are of spirit nature and origin. Though invisible to mortals, they perceive you as you are in the flesh without the aid of transformers or translators; they intellectually understand the mode of mortal life, and they share all of man's nonsensuous emotions and sentiments. They appreciate and greatly enjoy your efforts in music, art, and real humor. They are fully cognizant of your moral struggles and spiritual difficulties. They love human beings, and only good can result from your efforts to understand and love them." P38,S2,PP1,PG419

"While in personal status angels are not so far removed from human beings, in certain functional performances seraphim far transcend them. They possess many powers far beyond human comprehension. For example: You have been told that the "very hairs of your head are numbered," and it is true they are, but a seraphim does not spend her time counting them and keeping the number corrected up to date. Angels possess inherent and automatic (that is, automatic as far as you could perceive) powers of knowing such things; you would truly regard a seraphim as a mathematical prodigy. Therefore, numerous duties which would be tremendous tasks for mortals are performed with exceeding ease by seraphim." P38,S2,PP3,PG419

"Angels are superior to you in spiritual status, but they are not your judges or accusers." P38,S2,PP4,PG419

"You do well to love them, but you should not adore them; angels are not objects of worship." P38,S2,PP5,PG419

"The human race was created just a little lower than the more simple types of the angelic orders." P113,S7,PP3,PG1248

"Angels do not invade the sanctity of the human mind; they do not manipulate the will of mortals; neither do they directly contact with the indwelling Adjusters. The guardian of destiny influences you in every possible manner consistent with the dignity of your personality; under no circumstances do these angels interfere with the free action of the human will. Neither angels nor any other order of universe personality have power or authority to curtail or abridge the prerogatives of human choosing." P113,S5,PP1,PG1245

"Seraphim function as teachers of men by guiding the footsteps of the human personality into paths of new and progressive experiences. To accept the guidance of a seraphim rarely means attaining a life of ease. In following this leading you are sure to encounter, and if you have the courage, to traverse, the rugged hills of moral choosing and spiritual progress." P113,S4,PP3,PG1245

"Tempt not the angels of your supervision to lead you in troublous ways as a loving discipline designed to save your ease-drifting souls." P178,S1,PP10,PG1931 [Jesus speaking to about 50 of his followers on Sonship and Citizenship.]

f.   *Co-ordinated Ministry*

God is self-distributive. The various ministries discussed in this chapter spring from various attributes of God. God is divinely one, so the various ministries available to an individual from various attributes of God are divinely coordinated. For example, you won't find guidance of the Infinite Spirit in conflict with the guidance of the Father or the Creator Son.

"There are many spiritual influences, and they are all as one." P8,S5,PP4,PG95

g.   *Midwayers*

Midwayers are unseen planetary inhabitants, who further the cause of goodness here on Earth. They function in various roles.

"Most of the inhabited worlds of Nebadon [our local universe] harbor one or more groups of unique beings existing on a life-functioning level about midway between those of the mortals of the realms and of the angelic orders; hence are they called midway creatures. They appear to be an accident of time, but they occur so widespreadly and are so valuable as helpers that we have all long since accepted them as one of the essential orders of our combined planetary ministry.

On Urantia there function two distinct orders of midwayers: the primary or senior corps, ... and the secondary or younger group ..." P77,PP1,PG855

"Primary midwayers resemble angels more than mortals; the secondary orders are much more like human beings." P38,S9,PP8,PG424

"In the contacts made with the mortal beings of the material worlds, such as with the subject through whom these communications were transmitted, the midway creatures are always employed. They are an essential factor in such liaisons of the spiritual and the material levels." P77,S8,PP11,PG865

"The 1,111 loyal secondary midwayers are engaged in important missions on earth. As compared with their primary associates, they are decidedly material. They exist just outside the range of mortal vision and possess sufficient latitude of adaptation to make, at will, physical contact with what humans call "material things." These unique creatures have certain definite powers over the things of time and space, not excepting the beasts of the realm." P77,S8,PP11,PG865

"Material accidents, commonplace occurrences of a physical nature, are not arbitrarily interfered with by celestial personalities. Under ordinary circumstances only midway creatures can intervene in material conditions to safeguard the persons of men and women of destiny, and even in special situations these beings can so act only in obedience to the specific mandates of their superiors." P123,S4,PP7,PG1361

"Many of the more literal phenomena ascribed to angels have been performed by the secondary midway creatures." P77,S8,PP12,PG865

"It was the work of this secondary group, ably seconded by certain of the primary corps, that brought about the co-ordination of personalities and circumstances on Urantia which finally induced the planetary celestial supervisors to initiate those petitions that resulted in the granting of the mandates making possible the series of revelations of which this presentation is a part. But it should be made clear that the midway creatures are not involved in the sordid performances taking place under the general designation of "spiritualism." The midwayers at present on Urantia, all of whom are of honorable standing, are not connected with the phenomena of so-called "mediumship"; and they do not, ordinarily, permit humans to witness their sometimes necessary physical activities or other contacts with the material world, as they are perceived by human senses." P77,S8,PP13,PG865

We can thank midwayers for causing *The Urantia Book* revelation to be here.

"As actual citizens of Urantia, the midwayers have a kinship interest in the destiny of this sphere. They are a determined association, persistently working for the progress

of their native planet. Their determination is suggested by the motto of their order: "What the United Midwayers undertake, the United Midwayers do.""
P77,S9,PP3,PG866

CHAPTER 11: LIFE AFTER DEATH

In your material body, your are experiencing your first life on your planet of nativity, Urantia (Earth). It might be considered a shakedown cruise. Here you formulate your choices (consciously or unconsciously) for continuing your life after physical death.

Your material body is biologically determined through evolution and the choices of your ancestors. Your personality is a gift of God.

The divine Monitor, a fragment of God, your Thought Adjuster, dwells within you. Consciously or unconsciously you are choosing with or against God; the indwelling God is working with you to lead you Godward. God has attributes like love, understanding, truth, beauty, goodness, compassion, mercy, service, progress, etc. If you choose to co-operate with God, one way or another, consciously or unconsciously, or if you are even still capable of recognizing God, your life continues after your physical death.

Every time you make choices in cooperation with God, you are creating your soul. Your soul is real, but not either spiritual or material. It is "morontial," between the material and spiritual.

> "*Morontia* is a term designating a vast level intervening between the material and the spiritual. It may designate personal or impersonal realities, living or nonliving energies. The warp of morontia is spiritual; its woof is physical."
> FOREWORD,SV,PP12,PG9

Your soul and personality are the "you" that survives physical death. You are reborn in morontia form on one of the "mansion worlds," which are some of the architecturalized headquarters worlds of our local system, Satania. (About 1,000 inhabited planets make up an administrative unit called a system.) A diagram of our local system headquarters is presented on the following page.

And, for fun, allow me to insert another quick sketch of our local system headquarters, via the following quotes:

> "The administrative center of Satania consists of a cluster of architectural spheres, fifty-seven in number—Jerusem itself, the seven major satellites, and the forty-nine subsatellites. Jerusem, the system capital, is almost one hundred times the size of Urantia, although its gravity is a trifle less. Jerusem's major satellites are the seven transition worlds, each of which is about ten times as large as Urantia, while the seven subsatellites of these transition spheres are just about the size of Urantia.
>
> The seven mansion worlds are the seven subsatellites of transition world number one." P45,PP1,PG509
>
> "On Jerusem you will miss the rugged mountain ranges of Urantia and other

Chapter 11
78

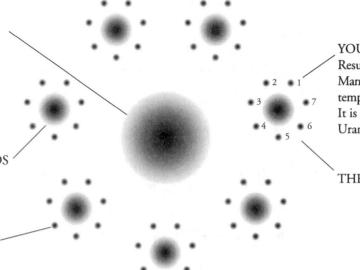

JERUSEM — the headquarters of our local system of 619 inhabited planets. It is about 100 times the size of earth.

"…the system headquarters is truly the heaven visualized by the majority of twentieth-century religious believers." 46:0

THE SEVEN TRANSITION WORLDS
Each is about 10 times the size of earth. These are the seven primary satellites around Jerusem.

The 49 subsatellites, each about the size of earth.

"…The entire system of 57 architecturalized worlds is independently lighted, heated, watered, and energized…" 45:0

YOU ARE RESURRECTED HERE!
Resurrection hall is on the First Mansion World. It is "…the enormous temple of personality assembly." 47:3 It is there you are resurrected. The Urantia Book explains much more.

THE SEVEN MANSION WORLDS

"On the mansion worlds the resurrected mortal survivors resume their lives just where they left off when overtaken by death." 47:0

"Almost the entire experience of mansion world number one pertains to deficiency ministry. Survivors arriving on this first of the detention spheres present so many and such varied defects of creature character and deficience of mortal experience that the major activities of the realm are occupied with the correction and cure of these manifold legacies of the life in the flesh on the material evolutionary worlds of time and space." 47:3 You continue to improve and progress through the 57 system worlds. Then you graduate from the system headquarters, and go to our constellation headquarters (one constellation =100 systems).

"Though you have morontia bodies, you continue, through all seven of these worlds [The Seven Mansion Worlds], to eat, drink, and rest. You partake of the morontia order of food, a kingdom of living energy unknown on the material worlds. Both food and water are fully utilized in the morontia body; there is no residual waste…" 47:4

Administrative Center of Satania, Our Local System

A limited conceptual interpretation based on The Urantia Book revelation. All quotes are from The Urantia Book
47:4 refers to Paper 47, Section 4
Not to Scale

> evolved worlds since there are neither earthquakes nor rainfalls, but you will enjoy the beauteous highlands and other unique variations of topography and landscape. Enormous areas of Jerusem are preserved in a "natural state," and the grandeur of such districts is quite beyond the powers of human imagination." P46,S2,PP1,PG520

> "Jerusem is indeed a foretaste of paradisiacal glory and grandeur. But you can never hope to gain an adequate idea of these glorious architectural worlds by any attempted description. There is so little that can be compared with aught on your world, and even then the things of Jerusem so transcend the things of Urantia that the comparison is almost grotesque. Until you actually arrive on Jerusem, you can hardly entertain anything like a true concept of the heavenly worlds, ..." P46,S2,PP6,PG521

You make, usually here on Earth, choices that demonstrate your wish to survive and continue. Then you are resurrected in morontia form, where your continued choices for attunement with God confirm your survival decisions, eventually resulting in fusion with your indwelling divine Monitor (which actually is the divine you). At this point, you become spiritual, and your Adjuster or Monitor gains personality. Until fusion, you can choose away from God. Once you fuse, your ascendant career truly begins.

> "... at any time before fusion with the Adjuster the evolving and ascending creature can choose to forsake the will of the Paradise Father. Fusion with the Adjuster signalizes the fact that the ascending mortal has eternally and unreservedly chosen to do the Father's will." P111,S3,PP1,PG1219

Although it has been relatively rare thus far on our planet, humans can fuse with their divine Monitors or Adjusters during their first short life in the flesh.

> "This fusion during physical life instantly consumes the material body; the human beings who might witness such a spectacle would only observe the translating mortal disappear "in chariots of fire."" P110,S7,PP2,PG1212

It is possible to choose away from God. And I imagine this means chronically choosing things like hate, deceit, egotism, ugliness, pride, resentment, bigotry, badness, immorality, disservice and disloyalty to others, and rejection of the leadings of God within.

You choose, you are not coerced. You are fairly adjudicated by high-order superuniverse beings called Ancients of Days (a superuniverse contains about one trillion inhabited planets).

Those who have chosen to reject God, to the point where they are judged to have no survival value, are undone; they are made as if they never were. Certain attributes of them become part of God the Supreme, which is an evolutionary attribute of God. God is not vindictive, those who choose away are not punished eternally.

Those who have survival value progress and ascend upward and inward through the universe of universes, to eventually "sit at the right hand of the Father", before going back out to do service in the universes, as an order of beings called finaliters.

The Urantia Book explains the survival process in much greater detail. When you die, you are unconscious until resurrected. Your memory records are in the keeping of the fragment of God that has indwelt you, and your soul is in keeping of appropriate seraphim. Your resurrection includes the reunion of your Adjuster and your soul. Your soul, which you created over your life by making choices in co-operation with the indwelling Adjuster, and your personality, are resurrected.

When you are resurrected, you begin life again right where you left off, except you are in different form. As you progress through all seven mansion worlds, you are trained, and deficiencies are corrected.

> "As to the chances of mortal survival, let it be made forever clear: All souls of every possible phase of mortal existence will survive provided they manifest willingness to co-operate with their indwelling Adjusters and exhibit a desire to find God and to attain divine perfection, even though these desires be but the first faint flickers of the primitive comprehension of that "true light which lights every man who comes into the world."" P40,S5,PP16,PG447

> "... a mercy credit is established for the survival of each rational creature, a credit of lavish proportions and one of sufficient grace to insure the survival of every soul who really desires divine citizenship." P28,S6,PP5,PG314

> "If ever there is doubt as to the advisability of advancing a human identity to the mansion worlds, the universe governments invariably rule in the personal interests of that individual; they unhesitatingly advance such a soul to the status of a transitional being, while they continue their observations of the emerging morontia intent and spiritual purpose. Thus divine justice is certain of achievement, and divine mercy is accorded further opportunity for extending its ministry." P112,S5,PP7,PG1233

> "Mortal man may draw near God and may repeatedly forsake the divine will so long as the power of choice remains. Man's final doom is not sealed until he has lost the power to choose the Father's will. There is never a closure of the Father's heart to the need and the petition of his children. Only do his offspring close their hearts forever to the Father's drawing power when they finally and forever lose the desire to do his divine will—to know him and to be like him." P5,S1,PP11,PG64

> "Of all the dangers which beset man's mortal nature and jeopardize his spiritual integrity, pride is the greatest. Courage is valorous, but egotism is vainglorious and suicidal. Reasonable self-confidence is not to be deplored. Man's ability to transcend himself is the one thing which distinguishes him from the animal kingdom.
> Pride is deceitful, intoxicating, and sin-breeding whether found in an individual, a group, a race, or a nation. It is literally true, "Pride goes before a fall."" P111,S6,PP10,PG1223

> "Make not the mistake of estimating the soul's worth by the imperfections of the mind or by the appetites of the body. Judge not the soul nor evaluate its destiny by the standard of a single unfortunate human episode. Your spiritual destiny is conditioned only by your spiritual longings and purposes." P156,S5,PP9,PG1739

> "Undiluted evil, complete error, willful sin, and unmitigated iniquity are inherently and automatically suicidal." P2,S3,PP5,PG37

In summary, evil is an unconscious or unintended transgression of the divine law (God's will), sin is a knowing, conscious transgression, and iniquity consists of purposeful and persistent transgressions.

"Law is life itself and not the rules of its conduct. Evil is a transgression of law, not a violation of the rules of conduct pertaining to life, which is the law." P48,S6,PP23,PG555

"Salvation should be taken for granted by those who believe in the fatherhood of God. The believer's chief concern should not be the selfish desire for personal salvation but rather the unselfish urge to love and, therefore, serve one's fellows even as Jesus loved and served mortal men." P188,S4,PP9,PG2017

"The mortals of the realms will arise in the morning of the resurrection with the same type of transition or morontia body that Jesus had when he arose from the tomb on this Sunday morning. These bodies do not have circulating blood, and such beings do not partake of ordinary material food; nevertheless, these morontia forms are real." P190,PP3,PG2029

"... the real and conscious reassembly of actual and complete personality takes place in the resurrection halls of mansonia number one. Throughout all eternity you will recall the profound memory impressions of your first witnessing of these resurrection mornings.

From the resurrection halls you proceed to the Melchizedek sector, where you are assigned permanent residence. Then you enter upon ten days of personal liberty. You are free to explore the immediate vicinity of your new home and to familiarize yourself with the program which lies immediately ahead. You also have time to gratify your desire to consult the registry and call upon your loved ones and other earth friends who may have preceded you to these worlds. At the end of your ten-day period of leisure you begin the second step in the Paradise journey, for the mansion worlds are actual training spheres, not merely detention planets." P47,S3,PP6,PG533 [Mansonia number one is one of the mansion worlds at the headquarters of our local system.]

"On mansion world number one (or another in case of advanced status) you will resume your intellectual training and spiritual development at the exact level whereon they were interrupted by death. Between the time of planetary death or translation and resurrection on the mansion world, mortal man gains absolutely nothing aside from experiencing the fact of survival. You begin over there right where you leave off down here.

Almost the entire experience of mansion world number one pertains to deficiency ministry. Survivors arriving on this first of the detention spheres present so many and such varied defects of creature character and deficiencies of mortal experience that the major activities of the realm are occupied with the correction and cure of these manifold legacies of the life in the flesh on the material evolutionary worlds of time and space." P47,S3,PP7,PG533

"And throughout all of these successive ages and stages of evolutionary growth, there is one part of you that remains absolutely unaltered, and that is personality—permanence in the presence of change." P112,PP1,PG1225

CHAPTER 12: WHO JESUS WAS, WHAT HE DID, AND EXCERPTS FROM HIS LIFE AND TEACHINGS

The last section of *The Urantia Book* is titled The Life and Teachings of Jesus. His teachings are re-presented in modern phraseology. Consequently, presentations of Jesus's teachings in *The Urantia Book* can seem dissimilar to those in the Bible, with which people are more familiar.

The Urantia Book presents the story of Jesus's life and teachings very well. I will present a small sampling of content, events, and teachings. Consequently, the following quotes will tend to jump from one topic, or one facet of his life, to another, and do not present the full story.

This chapter begins with a review, including some additional information about Jesus' bestowal.

a. Review

The Isle of Paradise is located in a perfect central universe, Havona, which is surrounded by seven, huge evolutionary superuniverses. Each of the seven superuniverses contain 100,000 local universes. These local universes are created by Creator Sons accompanied by Creative Daughters of the Infinite Spirit, both of whom are of God, and from Paradise. Each local universe, when mature, will contain 100 constellations, each constellation will contain 100 systems, and each system will contain 1,000 inhabited planets. Thus each local universe contains about 10,000,000 inhabited planets.

We mortals, humans, created by evolutionary techniques on planets, are the "... lowest creature life of will endowment." P35,S2,PP1,PG385. As planets evolve, they are periodically given bestowals or gifts, which are revelations of truth, to aid in the planetary evolution to light and life. Our planet has had five of these revelations: the first three were the Planetary Prince, Adam and Eve, and Machiventa Melchizedek, the fourth was Jesus Christ, and the fifth *The Urantia Book*.

Usually, when a planet is fairly well evolved toward light and life, "When the worlds have become ripe for spiritualization, ..." P52,S5,PP2,PG595, and not "... until the races have ascended to the highest levels of intellectual development and ethical attainment ...", P52,S5,PP1,PG595 they receive a Paradise Bestowal Son, a representative of Paradise. This representative of Paradise is an Avonal Son, except "... once in each local universe, ..." P52,S5,PP2,PG595 when the local universe Creator Son, who is also from Paradise, fulfills this role. When this bestowal is completed, the Spirit of Truth is poured out on the flesh. After the Spirit of Truth arrives, all normal minded humans receive Thought Adjusters, those indwelling fragments of the Heavenly Father.

Our Paradise Bestowal Son was Jesus Christ, God in man. Creator Sons are of the order of Michaels, our local universe is named Nebadon, so our local universe Creator Son is named Michael of Nebadon. Jesus Christ was a human incarnation of our local universe Creator Son, Michael of Nebadon, or Christ Michael.

I include the following descriptive quote about the Isle of Paradise, because Jesus was/is a Paradise representative. Personally, I think the word Christ connotes "Paradise representative". Paradise is a very high place:

> "Paradise is the eternal center of the universe of universes and the abiding place of the Universal Father, the Eternal Son, the Infinite Spirit, and their divine co-ordinates and associates. This central Isle is the most gigantic organized body of cosmic reality in all the master universe. Paradise is a material sphere as well as a spiritual abode. All of the intelligent creation of the Universal Father is domiciled on material abodes; hence must the absolute controlling center also be material, literal. And again it should be reiterated that spirit things and spiritual beings are *real*.

> "The material beauty of Paradise consists in the magnificence of its physical perfection; the grandeur of the Isle of God is exhibited in the superb intellectual accomplishments and mind development of its inhabitants; the glory of the central Isle is shown forth in the infinite endowment of divine spirit personality— the light of life. But the depths of the spiritual beauty and the wonders of this magnificent ensemble are utterly beyond the comprehension of the finite mind of material creatures. The glory and spiritual splendor of the divine abode are impossible of mortal comprehension. And Paradise is from eternity; there are neither records nor traditions respecting the origin of this nuclear Isle of Light and Life." P11,PP1,PG118

b.   *Additional Perspective*

Creator Sons, to obtain full and unlimited sovereignty over their created local universes, are mandated by the Paradise Father to undergo seven bestowals of themselves, as seven different orders or types of beings they have created in their local universe, in order to gain creature experience:

> "To live such identical lives as he imposes upon the intelligent beings of his own creation, thus to bestow himself in the likeness of his various orders of created beings, is a part of the price which every Creator Son must pay for the full and supreme sovereignty of his self-made universe of things and beings." P120,PP1,PG1323

So our local universe Creator Son, Michael, as well as being our Paradise Bestowal Son, was also fulfilling an incarnation mandate while he lived here as Jesus of Nazareth.

> "Before the events I am about to delineate, Michael of Nebadon had bestowed himself six times after the similitude of six differing orders of his diverse creation of intelligent beings. Then he prepared to descend upon Urantia in the likeness of mortal flesh, the lowest order of his intelligent will creatures, and, as such a human of the material realm, to execute the final act in the drama of the acquirement of universe sovereignty in accordance with the mandates of the divine Paradise Rulers of the universe of universes." P120,PP2,PG1323

> "Always be mindful of the twofold purpose of Michael's Bestowal on Urantia:
>
> 1. The mastering of the experience of living the full life of a human creature in mortal flesh, the completion of his sovereignty in Nebadon.
> 2. The revelation of the Universal Father to the mortal dwellers on the worlds of time and space and the more effective leading of these same mortals to a better understanding of the Universal Father." P128,PP2,PG1407

Who Jesus Was, What He Did, and Excerpts from His Life and Teachings

Of the seven incarnations that Creator Sons do, they do one under the divine will of each of the seven possible combinations of the Paradise Trinity: that is, one each under the Father, Son, and Spirit, one each under the Father-Son, Son-Spirit, and Father-Spirit, and one under the Father-Son-Spirit. Jesus's life on this planet was his incarnation dedicated to the Father's will.

Immanuel, also from Paradise, is a Paradise Trinity advisor and counselor upon request, to Michael. Immanuel presented the seventh bestowal commission to Michael. Here's some excerpts from that presentation that help us understand Jesus' gift to our planet:

> "Now you are about to appear upon Urantia, the disordered and disturbed planet of your choice, not as a fully developed mortal, but as a helpless babe. This, my comrade, will be a new and untried experience for you." P120,S1,PP1,PG1325

> "Throughout your Urantia bestowal you need be concerned with but one thing, the unbroken communion between you and your Paradise Father; and it will be by the perfection of such a relationship that the world of your bestowal, even all the universe of your creation, will behold a new and more understandable revelation of your Father and my Father, the Universal Father of all." P120,S1,PP4,PG1326

> "You may proceed upon your mission with but a single thought—the enhanced revelation of our Father to the intelligent beings of your universe." P120,S1,PP5,PG1326

> "... you will also so function as to make a new revelation of man to God." P120,S2,PP8,PG1328

> "I caution you ever to bear in mind that, while in fact you are to become an ordinary human of the realm, in potential you will remain a Creator Son of the Paradise Father. Throughout this incarnation, although you will live and act as a Son of Man, the creative attributes of your personal divinity will follow you from Salvington to Urantia." P120,S2,PP9,PG1329 [Salvington is the headquarters sphere of our local universe. I think many of the "miracles" associated with Jesus's life are attributable to these creative attributes of his personal divinity.]

> "... you also give some attention to the realization and exemplification of some things practical and immediately helpful to your fellow men." P120,S3,PP2,PG1329 [At one point Jesus improved the design of boats.]

The writers of *The Urantia Book* were able to re-present the historic record of Jesus' life because there are universe records.

> "Every occurrence of significance in the organized and inhabited creation is a matter of record. While events of no more than local importance find only a local recording, those of wider significance are dealt with accordingly." P25,S5,PP3,PG281

There are seraphic (angelic) recorders:

> "This enormous corps of recorders busy themselves with keeping straight the record of each mortal [including Jesus] of time from the moment of birth up through the universe career until such an individual either leaves Salvington for the superuniverse regime or is "blotted out of recorded existence" by the mandate of the Ancients of

Chapter 12

Days." P37,S3,PP7,PG409 [Salvington is our local universe headquarters, and Ancients of Days are superuniverse adjudicators.]

This recorded information is the extrahuman information mentioned in the following quote. The following is part of an explanation written by the secondary midwayer who provided the basis for the narrative of the life and teachings of Jesus.

> "The memoranda which I have collected, and from which I have prepared this narrative of the life and teachings of Jesus—aside from the memory of the record of the Apostle Andrew—embrace thought gems and superior concepts of Jesus' teachings assembled from more than two thousand human beings who have lived on earth from the days of Jesus down to the time of the inditing of these revelations, more correctly restatements. The revelatory permission has been utilized only when the human record and human concepts failed to supply an adequate thought pattern. My revelatory commission forbade me to resort to extrahuman sources of either information or expression until such a time as I could testify that I had failed in my efforts to find the required conceptual expression in purely human sources." P121,S8,PP13,PG1343

As already discussed, Jesus was an incarnation of our local universe Creator Son, Michael of Nebadon, acting as our planet's Paradise Bestowal Son.

> "Christ Michael did not progressively become God. God did not, at some vital moment in the earth life of Jesus, become man. Jesus was God *and* man—always and even forevermore. And this God and this man were, and now are, *one*, even as the Paradise Trinity of three beings is in reality *one* Deity.
>
> Never lose sight of the fact that the supreme spiritual purpose of the Michael bestowal was to enhance the *revelation of God*.
>
> Urantia mortals have varying concepts of the miraculous, but to us who live as citizens of the local universe there are few miracles, and of these by far the most intriguing are the incarnational bestowals of the Paradise Sons. The appearance in and on your world, by apparently natural processes, of a divine Son, we regard as a miracle—the operation of universal laws beyond our understanding. Jesus of Nazareth was a miraculous person.
>
> In and through all this extraordinary experience, God the Father chose to manifest himself as he always does—*in the usual way*—in the normal, natural, and dependable way of divine acting." P120,S4,PP3,PG1331

> "... Michael finally chose Urantia as the planet whereon to enact his final bestowal. Subsequent to this decision Gabriel [see below] made a personal visit to Urantia, and, as a result of his study of human groups and his survey of the spiritual, intellectual, racial, and geographic features of the world and its peoples, he decided that the Hebrews possessed those relative advantages which warranted their selection as the bestowal race." P122,PP2,PG1344

c. **Announcements**

> "Of all couples living in Palestine at about the time of Michael's projected bestowal, Joseph and Mary possessed the most ideal combination of widespread racial connections and superior average of personality endowments. It was the plan of Michael

to appear on earth as an *average* man, that the common people might understand him and receive him; wherefore Gabriel selected just such persons as Joseph and Mary to become the bestowal parents." P122,S1,PP3,PG1345

Gabriel is an order of being called a Bright and Morning Star, and there is only one in each local universe. They come from a union of the local universe Creator Son and the local universe Creative Mother Spirit, and act as chief executives for Creator Sons in local universes.

Gabriel appeared to Jesus's parents, and to John the Baptist's parents, to let them know their children were to be special workers for the Heavenly Father.

> "This vision greatly frightened Elizabeth [John the Baptist's mom.] After Gabriel's departure, she turned this experience over in her mind, long pondering the sayings of the majestic visitor, but did not speak of the revelation to anyone save her husband until her subsequent visit with Mary in early February of the following year." P122,S2,PP4,PG1345

> "One evening about sundown, before Joseph had returned home, Gabriel appeared to Mary by the side of a low stone table and, after she had recovered her composure, said: "I come at the bidding of one who is my Master and whom you shall love and nurture. To you, Mary, I bring glad tidings when I announce that the conception within you is ordained by heaven, and that in due time you will become the mother of a son; you shall call him Joshua, and he shall inaugurate the kingdom of heaven on earth and among men. Speak not of this matter save to Joseph and to Elizabeth, your kinswoman, to whom I have also appeared, and who shall presently also bear a son, whose name shall be John, and who will prepare the way for the message of deliverance which your son shall proclaim to men with great power and deep conviction. And doubt not my word, Mary, for this home has been chosen as the mortal habitat of the child of destiny. My benediction rests upon you, the power of the Most Highs will strengthen you, and the Lord of all the earth shall overshadow you." P122,S3,PP1,PG1346 [Most Highs are local universe sons of God who act as constellation Fathers/administrators.]

> "Gabriel's announcement to Mary was made the day following the conception of Jesus and was the only event of supernatural occurrence connected with her entire experience of carrying and bearing the child of promise." P122,S3,PP4,PG1347

d. Birth

> "All that night Mary was restless so that neither of them slept much. By the break of day the pangs of childbirth were well in evidence, and at noon, August 21, 7 B.C., with the help and kind ministrations of women fellow travelers, Mary was delivered of a male child. Jesus of Nazareth was born into the world, was wrapped in the clothes which Mary had brought along for such a possible contingency, and laid in a near-by manger.
>
> In just the same manner as all babies before that day and since have come into the world, the promised child was born; and on the eighth day, according to the Jewish practice, he was circumcised and formally named Joshua (Jesus)." P122,S8,PP1,PG1351

"These wise men saw no star to guide them to Bethlehem. The beautiful legend of the star of Bethlehem originated in this way: Jesus was born August 21 at noon, 7 B.C. On May 29, 7 B.C., there occurred an extraordinary conjunction of Jupiter and Saturn in the constellation of Pisces. And it is a remarkable astronomic fact that similar conjunctions occurred on September 29 and December 5 of the same year. Upon the basis of these extraordinary but wholly natural events the well-meaning zealots of the succeeding generation constructed the appealing legend of the star of Bethlehem and the adoring Magi led thereby to the manger, where they beheld and worshiped the newborn babe." P122,S8,PP7,PG1352

e. *Herod's Attempt*

Herod ordered "...that all boy babies under two years of age should be killed. In this manner he hoped to make sure that this child who was to become "king of the Jews" would be destroyed. And thus perished in one day sixteen boy babies in Bethlehem of Judea. But intrigue and murder, even in his own immediate family, were common occurrences at the court of Herod.

The massacre of these infants took place about the middle of October, 6 B.C., when Jesus was a little over one year of age. But there were believers in the coming Messiah even among Herod's court attachés, and one of these, learning of the order to slaughter the Bethlehem boy babies, communicated with Zacharias, who in turn dispatched a messenger to Joseph; and the night before the massacre Joseph and Mary departed from Bethlehem with the babe for Alexandria in Egypt. ... They sojourned in Alexandria two full years, not returning to Bethlehem until after the death of Herod. P122,S10,PP3,PG1354 [This was the first Herod in Jesus' life. The second was Herod Antipas, the son of Herod.]

f. *Family Life*

"From the time Jesus was five years old until he was ten, he was one continuous question mark. While Joseph and Mary could not always answer his questions, they never failed fully to discuss his inquiries and in every other possible way to assist him in his efforts to reach a satisfactory solution of the problem which his alert mind had suggested." P123,S2,PP3,PG1358

"Though Joseph was now assuming the direct responsibility for Jesus' intellectual and religious education, his mother still interested herself in his home training. She taught him to know and care for the vines and flowers growing about the garden walls which completely surrounded the home plot. She also provided on the roof of the house (the summer bedroom) shallow boxes of sand in which Jesus worked out maps and did much of his early practice at writing Aramaic, Greek, and later on, Hebrew, for in time he learned to read, write, and speak, fluently, all three languages." P123,S2,PP7,PG1358

"Though Joseph and Mary often talked about the future of their eldest child, had you been there, you would only have observed the growing up of a normal, healthy, carefree, but exceedingly inquisitive child of that time and place." P123,S2,PP9,PG1359

"Next, in addition to his more formal schooling, Jesus began to make contact with human nature from the four quarters of the earth as men from many lands passed in and out of his father's repair shop. When he grew older, he mingled freely with the caravans as they tarried near the spring for rest and nourishment. Being a fluent speaker of Greek, he had little trouble in conversing with the majority of the caravan travelers and conductors." P123,S5,PP6,PG1362

"Throughout his years at the synagogue he was a brilliant student, possessing a great advantage since he was conversant with three languages. The Nazareth chazan, on the occasion of Jesus' finishing the course in his school, remarked to Joseph that he feared he "had learned more from Jesus' searching questions" than he had "been able to teach the lad." P123,S5,PP9,PG1363

"Late this year he had a fishing experience of two months with his uncle on the Sea of Galilee, and he was very successful. Before attaining manhood, he had become an expert fisherman." P124,S2,PP7,PG1369

When Jesus was thirteen, he went to his first passover at the temple in Jerusalem with his family. This was a thrilling experience for him, "... and it long stood out in his memory as the great event of his later childhood and early youth." P125,PP1,PG1377 In the night, just before they arrived, for the first time in his human life, he had a supernatural experience. A messenger from Salvington, commissioned by Immanuel, appeared to him saying "The hour has come. It is time that you began to be about your Father's business." P124,S6,PP15,PG1376

Arriving at the temple, he was shocked by irreverent sights and sounds in the temple courts, including the buying and selling of sacrificial animals, cursing, loud talking, and painted courtesans. At the priest's court, at the alter, he became sickened from the killing of sacrificial animals and the blood. His father wisely took him away to see the "gate beautiful".

He enjoyed the temple discussions. After attending the seven-day Passover ceremonies, it came time for the family to leave. Jesus was occupied, in the temple, absorbed in a discussion about angels, and mindless of time. Mary left for home with a group of women, Joseph with a group of men. His parents traveled for nearly a day before missing him, then came back to Jerusalem but did not soon find him. Jesus was occupied, participating in temple discussions, unmindful of his parents, and staying with family friends at night. His parents found him in the temple on the fourth day following their separation. They had not thought to look inside the temple, in the discussion groups. The evening before they found him, they "...had heard about this strange youth who so deftly sparred with the expounders of the law, but it had not occurred to them that this lad was their son." P125,S6,PP4,PG1383

During this time in the temple, he was actually teaching by sincerely and skillfully asking questions that would challenge an existing teaching, and convey his own. He had made quite an impact, with the many penetrating questions he asked, such as "If God is a father who loves his children, why all this slaughter of animals to gain the divine favor - has the teaching of Moses been misunderstood?" and "Since the temple is dedicated to the worship of the Father in Heaven, is it consistent to permit the presence of those who engage in secular barter and trade?" P125,S5,PP5,PG1382

When his parents finally found him in a discussion group, he responded to their public expression of distress by saying "Why is it you have so long sought me? Would you not expect to find me in my Father's house since the time has come when I should be about my Father's business?" The others withdrew. Then, alone with his parents, he said "Come, my parents, none has done aught but that which he thought best. Our Father in heaven has ordained these things; let us depart for home." P125,S6,PP7&PP8,PG1384

Back to various quotes:

> "This is the calendar year of his fourteenth birthday. He had become a good yoke maker and worked well with both canvas and leather. He was also rapidly developing into an expert carpenter and cabinetmaker. This summer he made frequent trips to the top of the hill to the northwest of Nazareth for prayer and meditation. He was gradually becoming more self-conscious of the nature of his bestowal on earth." P126,S1,PP1,PG1387

> "All did go well until that fateful day of Tuesday, September 25, when a runner from Sepphoris brought to this Nazareth home the tragic news that Joseph had been severely injured by the falling of a derrick while at work on the governor's residence. ... But Joseph died of his injuries before Mary arrived. They brought him to Nazareth, and on the following day he was laid to rest with his fathers.
>
> Just at the time when prospects were good and the future looked bright, an apparently cruel hand struck down the head of this Nazareth household, the affairs of this home were disrupted, and every plan for Jesus and his future education was demolished. This carpenter lad, now just past fourteen years of age, awakened to the realization that he had not only to fulfill the commission of his heavenly Father to reveal the divine nature on earth and in the flesh, but that his young human nature must also shoulder the responsibility of caring for his widowed mother and seven brothers and sisters—and another yet to be born. This lad of Nazareth now became the sole support and comfort of this so suddenly bereaved family. Thus were permitted those occurrences of the natural order of events on Urantia which would force this young man of destiny so early to assume these heavy but highly educational and disciplinary responsibilities attendant upon becoming the head of a human family, of becoming father to his own brothers and sisters, of supporting and protecting his mother, of functioning as guardian of his father's home, the only home he was to know while on this world.
>
> Jesus cheerfully accepted the responsibilities so suddenly thrust upon him, and he carried them faithfully to the end. At least one great problem and anticipated difficulty in his life had been tragically solved—he would not now be expected to go to Jerusalem to study under the rabbis. It remained always true that Jesus "sat at no man's feet." He was ever willing to learn from even the humblest of little children, but he never derived authority to teach truth from human sources." P126,S2,PP1,PG1388

> "The economic affairs of the family continued to run fairly smoothly as there was quite a sum of money on hand at the time of Joseph's death. Jesus early demonstrated the possession of keen business judgment and financial sagacity. He was liberal but frugal; he was saving but generous. He proved to be a wise and efficient administrator of his father's estate." P126,S2,PP7,PG1389

> "The great confusion of Jesus' younger days now arose. Having settled something about the nature of his mission on earth, "to be about his Father's business"— to show

forth his Father's loving nature to all mankind—he began to ponder anew the many statements in the Scriptures referring to the coming of a national deliverer, a Jewish teacher or king. To what event did these prophecies refer? Was not he a Jew? or was he? Was he or was he not of the house of David? His mother averred he was; his father had ruled that he was not. He decided he was not. But had the prophets confused the nature and mission of the Messiah?

After all, could it be possible that his mother was right? In most matters, when differences of opinion had arisen in the past, she had been right. If he were a new teacher and not the Messiah, then how should he recognize the Jewish Messiah if such a one should appear in Jerusalem during the time of his earth mission; and, further, what should be his relation to this Jewish Messiah? And what should be his relation, after embarking on his life mission, to his family? to the Jewish commonwealth and religion? to the Roman Empire? to the gentiles and their religions? Each of these momentous problems this young Galilean turned over in his mind and seriously pondered while he continued to work at the carpenter's bench, laboriously making a living for himself, his mother, and eight other hungry mouths." P126,S3,PP10,PG1390

"The pay of a common day-laboring carpenter was slowly diminishing. By the end of this year Jesus could earn, by working early and late, only the equivalent of about twenty-five cents a day. By the next year they found it difficult to pay the civil taxes, not to mention the synagogue assessments and the temple tax of one-half shekel. During this year the tax collector tried to squeeze extra revenue out of Jesus, even threatening to take his harp." P126,S5,PP5,PG1393

"The great shock of his fifteenth year came when Jesus went over to Sepphoris to receive the decision of Herod [the second Herod, not the one that died shortly after Jesus' birth] regarding the appeal taken to him in the dispute about the amount of money due Joseph at the time of his accidental death. Jesus and Mary had hoped for the receipt of a considerable sum of money when the treasurer at Sepphoris had offered them a paltry amount. Joseph's brothers had taken an appeal to Herod himself, and now Jesus stood in the palace and heard Herod decree that his father had nothing due him at the time of his death. And for such an unjust decision Jesus never again trusted Herod Antipas. It is not surprising that he once alluded to Herod as "that fox.""
P126,S5,PP7,PG1393

"This physically strong and robust youth also acquired the full growth of his human intellect, not the full experience of human thinking but the fullness of capacity for such intellectual development. He possessed a healthy and well-proportioned body, a keen and analytical mind, a kind and sympathetic disposition, a somewhat fluctuating but aggressive temperament, all of which were becoming organized into a strong, striking, and attractive personality." P127,S1,PP3,PG1395

"As time went on, it became more difficult for his mother and his brothers and sisters to understand him; they stumbled over his sayings and misinterpreted his doings. They were all unfitted to comprehend their eldest brother's life because their mother had given them to understand that he was destined to become the deliverer of the Jewish people. After they had received from Mary such intimations as family secrets, imagine

their confusion when Jesus would make frank denials of all such ideas and intentions."
P127,S1,PP4,PG1396

"It was by just such wise and thoughtful planning that Jesus prepared the way for his eventual withdrawal from active participation in the affairs of his family."
P128,S2,PP7,PG1410

"The Son of Man had now made every preparation for detaching himself permanently from the Nazareth home; and this was not easy for him to do. Jesus naturally loved his people; he loved his family, and this natural affection had been tremendously augmented by his extraordinary devotion to them. The more fully we bestow ourselves upon our fellows, the more we come to love them; and since Jesus had given himself so fully to his family, he loved them with a great and fervent affection."
P129,PP2,PG1419

Jesus was the head of household, and didn't leave his family until he had installed James, his next youngest brother, in his place, and family affairs were in order and functioning well.

His experience also included the death of his baby brother Amos when he was 18, and he declined a sincere offer of marriage when he was 19.

g. *Adult Life, Prior to Public Ministry*

Jesus left his family, and worked and traveled for a number of years. He did not begin his public ministry until he was baptized by John. During this time he continued to develop increasing contact with God (his Thought Adjuster), and an increasing knowledge of who he was (a Creator Son) before he was incarnated as a human. To remain less conspicuous, Jesus segregated aspects of his life, knowing that a reputation could interfere with the teachings he wished to impart. He declined offers to head a school funded by rich people that was to outrival Alexandria, and another offer to become an established religious teacher in Alexandria. During this time he personally talked with, and ministered to, many people.

"Perhaps the most notable of all these contacts was the one with a young Hellenist named Stephen. This young man was on his first visit to Jerusalem and chanced to meet Jesus on Thursday afternoon of Passover week. While they both strolled about viewing the Asmonean palace, Jesus began the casual conversation that resulted in their becoming interested in each other, and which led to a four-hour discussion of the way of life and the true God and his worship. Stephen was tremendously impressed with what Jesus said; he never forgot his words.

And this was the same Stephen who subsequently became a believer in the teachings of Jesus, and whose boldness in preaching this early gospel resulted in his being stoned to death by irate Jews. Some of Stephen's extraordinary boldness in proclaiming his view of the new gospel was the direct result of this earlier interview with Jesus. But Stephen never even faintly surmised that the Galilean he had talked with some fifteen years previously was the very same person whom he later proclaimed the world's Savior, and for whom he was so soon to die, thus becoming the first martyr of the newly evolving Christian faith. When Stephen yielded up his life as the price of his attack upon the Jewish temple and its traditional practices, there stood by one named Saul, a citizen of Tarsus. And when Saul saw how this Greek could die for his faith, there were aroused in his heart those emotions which eventually led him to espouse the cause for which Stephen died; later on he became the aggressive and indomitable Paul, the philosopher, if not the sole founder, of the Christian religion." P128,S3,PP5,PG1411

"One purpose which Jesus had in mind, when he sought to segregate certain features of his earthly experience, was to prevent the building up of such a versatile and spectacular career as would cause subsequent generations to venerate the teacher in place of obeying the truth which he had lived and taught. Jesus did not want to build up such a human record of achievement as would attract attention from his teaching. Very early he recognized that his followers would be tempted to formulate a religion about him which might become a competitor of the gospel of the kingdom that he intended to proclaim to the world. Accordingly, he consistently sought to suppress everything during his eventful career which he thought might be made to serve this natural human tendency to exalt the teacher in place of proclaiming his teachings." P128,S4,PP6,PG1413

"The real purpose of his trip around the Mediterranean basin was to know men. He came very close to hundreds of humankind on this journey. He met and loved all manner of men, rich and poor, high and low, black and white, educated and uneducated, cultured and uncultured, animalistic and spiritual, religious and irreligious, moral and immoral." P129,S3,PP8,PG1424

"He talked with a Roman senator on politics and statesmanship, and this one contact with Jesus made such an impression on this legislator that he spent the rest of his life vainly trying to induce his colleagues to change the course of the ruling policy from the idea of the government supporting and feeding the people to that of the people supporting the government. Jesus spent one evening with a wealthy slaveholder, talked about man as a son of God, and the next day this man, Claudius, gave freedom to one hundred and seventeen slaves. He visited at dinner with a Greek physician, telling him that his patients had minds and souls as well as bodies, and thus led this able doctor to attempt a more far-reaching ministry to his fellow men. He talked with all sorts of people in every walk of life. The only place in Rome he did not visit was the public baths. He refused to accompany his friends to the baths because of the sex promiscuity which there prevailed." P132,S4,PP5,PG1461

h. *John the Baptist; The Beginning of Public Ministry*

Jesus' presented himself to John for baptism. John, as a preacher, had prepared the way for Jesus, preaching "the kingdom of God is at hand." Jesus' baptism began his four year public ministry to the world, which ended with his physical death.

"As John laid his hands upon Jesus to baptize him, the indwelling Adjuster took final leave of the perfected human soul of Joshua ben Joseph. And in a few moments this divine entity returned from Divinington [a sacred sphere of Paradise] as a Personalized Thought Adjuster and the chief of his kind throughout the entire local universe of Nebadon. Thus did Jesus observe his own former divine spirit descending on its return to him in personalized form. And he heard this same spirit of Paradise origin now speak, saying, "This is my beloved Son in whom I am well pleased." And John, with Jesus' two brothers, also heard these words. John's disciples, standing by the water's

edge, did not hear these words, neither did they see the apparition of the Personalized Adjuster. Only the eyes of Jesus beheld the Personalized Adjuster."
P136,S2,PP3,PG1511

> "When Jesus was baptized, he repented of no misdeeds; he made no confession of sin. His was the baptism of consecration to the performance of the will of the heavenly Father. At his baptism he heard the unmistakable call of his Father, the final summons to be about his Father's business, and he went away into private seclusion for forty days to think over these manifold problems. ...
>
> This day of baptism ended the purely human life of Jesus. The divine Son has found his Father, the Universal Father has found his incarnated Son, and they speak the one to the other.
>
> (Jesus was almost thirty-one and one-half years old when he was baptized. While Luke says that Jesus was baptized in the fifteenth year of the reign of Tiberius Caesar, which would be A.D. 29 since Augustus died in A.D. 14, it should be recalled that Tiberius was coemperor with Augustus for two and one-half years before the death of Augustus, having had coins struck in his honor in October, A.D. 11. The fifteenth year of his actual rule was, therefore, this very year of A.D. 26 that of Jesus' baptism. And this was also the year that Pontius Pilate began his rule as governor of Judea.)"
> P136,S2,PP6,PG1512

Not long after the baptism, John made "the memorable attack on Herod Antipas for unlawfully taking the wife of another man." P135,S10,PP2,PG1506 Herod then imprisoned John for this and other reasons. Herod held John in prison for over a year and a half. "Herod feared to release John lest he instigate rebellion. He feared to put him to death lest the multitude riot in the capital, for thousands of Pereans believed that John was a Holy Man, a prophet." P135,S12,PP2,PG1508

While drinking and socializing one evening, Herod promised anything to a young dancing woman. The young woman was the daughter of Herodias, Herod's unlawful wife, who hated John. The daughter asked the mom what to ask of Herod, and the mom directed the daughter to ask for the head of John the Baptist.

> "Herod was filled with fear and sorrow, but because of his oath and because of all those who sat at meat with him, he would not deny the request. And Herod Antipas sent a soldier, commanding him to bring the head of John. So was John that night beheaded in the prison, the soldier bringing the head of the prophet on a platter and presenting it to the young woman at the rear of the banquet hall. And the damsel gave the platter to her mother. When John's disciples heard of this, they came to the prison for the body of John, and after laying it in a tomb, they went and told Jesus."
> P135,S12,PP7,PG1508

i. *Examples of Jesus' Teachings and Attitudes*

> "Jesus frequently warned his listeners against covetousness, declaring that "a man's happiness consists not in the abundance of his material possessions." He constantly reiterated, "What shall it profit a man if he gain the whole world and lose his own soul?" He made no direct attack on the possession of property, but he did insist that it is eternally essential that spiritual values come first....And if Jesus were on earth today,

living his life in the flesh, he would be a great disappointment to the majority of good men and women for the simple reason that he would not take sides in present-day political, social, or economic disputes. He would remain grandly aloof while teaching you how to perfect your inner spiritual life so as to render you manyfold more competent to attack the solution of your purely human problems.

Jesus would make all men Godlike and then stand by sympathetically while these sons of God solve their own political, social, and economic problems. It was not wealth that he denounced, but what wealth does to the majority of its devotees. On this Thursday afternoon Jesus first told his associates that "it is more blessed to give than to receive."...P140,S8,PP17,PG1581

"Jesus did not attack the teachings of the Hebrew prophets or the Greek moralists. The Master recognized the many good things which these great teachers stood for, but he had come down to earth to teach something additional, "the voluntary conformity of man's will to God's will." Jesus did not want simply to produce a religious man, a mortal wholly occupied with religious feelings and actuated only by spiritual impulses. Could you have had but one look at him, you would have known that Jesus was a real man of great experience in the things of this world. The teachings of Jesus in this respect have been grossly perverted and much misrepresented all down through the centuries of the Christian era; you have also held perverted ideas about the Master's meekness and humility. What he aimed at in his life appears to have been a superb self-respect. He only advised man to humble himself that he might become truly exalted; what he really aimed at was true humility toward God. He placed great value upon sincerity—a pure heart. Fidelity was a cardinal virtue in his estimate of character, while courage was the very heart of his teachings. "Fear not" was his watchword, and patient endurance his ideal of strength of character. The teachings of Jesus constitute a religion of valor, courage, and heroism. And this is just why he chose as his personal representatives twelve commonplace men, the majority of whom were rugged, virile, and manly fishermen.

Jesus had little to say about the social vices of his day; seldom did he make reference to moral delinquency. He was a positive teacher of true virtue. He studiously avoided the negative method of imparting instruction; he refused to advertise evil. He was not even a moral reformer. He well knew, and so taught his apostles, that the sensual urges of mankind are not suppressed by either religious rebuke or legal prohibitions. His few denunciations were largely directed against pride, cruelty, oppression, and hypocrisy.

Jesus did not vehemently denounce even the Pharisees, as did John. He knew many of the scribes and Pharisees were honest of heart; he understood their enslaving bondage to religious traditions. Jesus laid great emphasis on "first making the tree good." He impressed the three [Peter, James, and John] that he valued the whole life, not just a certain few special virtues." P140,S8,PP20,PG1582

"But Jesus earnestly warned his apostles against the foolishness of the child of God who presumes upon the Father's love. He declared that the heavenly Father is not a lax, loose, or foolishly indulgent parent who is ever ready to condone sin and forgive recklessness. He cautioned his hearers not mistakenly to apply his illustrations of father and son so as to make it appear that God is like some overindulgent and unwise parents who conspire with the foolish of earth to encompass the moral undoing of their thoughtless children, and who are thereby certainly and directly contributing to the delinquency and early demoralization of their own offspring. Said Jesus: "My Father does not indulgently condone those acts and practices of his children which are self-destructive and suicidal to all moral growth and spiritual progress. Such sinful practices are an abomination in the sight of God." P147,S5,PP9,PG1653

He taught that

"... astrology is a mass of superstitious error which has no place in the gospel of the kingdom. ...

Divination, sorcery, and witchcraft are superstitions of ignorant minds, as also are the delusions of magic. ...

He exposed and denounced their belief in spells, ordeals, bewitching, cursing, signs, mandrakes, knotted cords, and all other forms of ignorant and enslaving superstition." P150,S3,PP3,PG1680

"At Edrei, where Thomas and his associates labored, Jesus spent a day and a night and, in the course of the evening's discussion, gave expression to the principles which should guide those who preach truth, and which should activate all who teach the gospel of the kingdom. Summarized and restated in modern phraseology, Jesus taught:

Always respect the personality of man. Never should a righteous cause be promoted by force; spiritual victories can be won only by spiritual power. This injunction against the employment of material influences refers to psychic force as well as to physical force. Overpowering arguments and mental superiority are not to be employed to coerce men and women into the kingdom. Man's mind is not to be crushed by the mere weight of logic or overawed by shrewd eloquence. While emotion as a factor in human decisions cannot be wholly eliminated, it should not be directly appealed to in the teachings of those who would advance the cause of the kingdom. Make your appeals directly to the divine spirit that dwells within the minds of men. Do not appeal to fear, pity, or mere sentiment. In appealing to men, be fair; exercise self-control and exhibit due restraint; show proper respect for the personalities of your pupils. Remember that I have said: "Behold, I stand at the door and knock, and if any man will open, I will come in."

In bringing men into the kingdom, do not lessen or destroy their self-respect. While overmuch self-respect may destroy proper humility and end in pride, conceit, and arrogance, the loss of self-respect often ends in paralysis of the will. It is the purpose of this gospel to restore self-respect to those who have lost it and to restrain it in those who have it. Make not the mistake of only condemning the wrongs in the lives of your pupils; remember also to accord generous recognition for the most praiseworthy things in their lives. Forget not that I will stop at nothing to restore self-respect to those who have lost it, and who really desire to regain it.

Take care that you do not wound the self-respect of timid and fearful souls. Do not indulge in sarcasm at the expense of my simple-minded brethren. Be not cynical with my fear-ridden children. Idleness is destructive of self-respect; therefore, admonish your brethren ever to keep busy at their chosen tasks, and put forth every effort to secure work for those who find themselves without employment.

Never be guilty of such unworthy tactics as endeavoring to frighten men and women into the kingdom. A loving father does not frighten his children into yielding obedience to his just requirements.

Sometime the children of the kingdom will realize that strong feelings of emotion are not equivalent to the leadings of the divine spirit. To be strongly and strangely impressed to do something or to go to a certain place, does not necessarily mean that such impulses are the leadings of the indwelling spirit.

Forewarn all believers regarding the fringe of conflict which must be traversed by all who pass from the life as it is lived in the flesh to the higher life as it is lived in the spirit. To those who live quite wholly within either realm, there is little conflict or confusion, but all are doomed to experience more or less uncertainty during the times of transition between the two levels of living. In entering the kingdom, you cannot escape its responsibilities or avoid its obligations, but remember: The gospel yoke is easy and the burden of truth is light.

The world is filled with hungry souls who famish in the very presence of the bread of life; men die searching for the very God who lives within them. Men seek for the treasures of the kingdom with yearning hearts and weary feet when they are all within the immediate grasp of living faith. Faith is to religion what sails are to a ship; it is an addition of power, not an added burden of life. There is but one struggle for those who enter the kingdom, and that is to fight the good fight of faith. The believer has only one battle, and that is against doubt— unbelief.

In preaching the gospel of the kingdom, you are simply teaching friendship with God. And this fellowship will appeal alike to men and women in that both will find that which most truly satisfies their characteristic longings and ideals. Tell my children that I am not only tender of their feelings and patient with their frailties, but that I am also ruthless with sin and intolerant of iniquity. I am indeed meek and humble in the presence of my Father, but I am equally and relentlessly inexorable where there is deliberate evildoing and sinful rebellion against the will of my Father in heaven.

You shall not portray your teacher as a man of sorrows. Future generations shall know also the radiance of our joy, the buoyancy of our good will, and the inspiration of our good humor. We proclaim a message of good news which is infectious in its transforming power. Our religion is throbbing with new life and new meanings. Those who accept this teaching are filled with joy and in their hearts are constrained to rejoice evermore. Increasing happiness is always the experience of all who are certain about God.

Teach all believers to avoid leaning upon the insecure props of false sympathy. You cannot develop strong characters out of the indulgence of self-pity; honestly endeavor to avoid the deceptive influence of mere fellowship in misery. Extend sympathy to the brave and courageous while you withhold overmuch pity from those cowardly souls who only halfheartedly stand up before the trials of living. Offer not consolation to those who lie down before their troubles without a struggle. Sympathize not with your fellows merely that they may sympathize with you in return.

When my children once become self-conscious of the assurance of the divine presence, such a faith will expand the mind, ennoble the soul, reinforce the personality, augment the happiness, deepen the spirit perception, and enhance the power to love and be loved.

Teach all believers that those who enter the kingdom are not thereby rendered immune to the accidents of time or to the ordinary catastrophes of nature. Believing the gospel will not prevent getting into trouble, but it will insure that you shall be unafraid when trouble does overtake you. If you dare to believe in me and wholeheartedly proceed to follow after me, you shall most certainly by so doing enter upon the sure pathway to trouble. I do not promise to deliver you from the waters of adversity, but I do promise to go with you through all of them.

And much more did Jesus teach this group of believers before they made ready for the night's sleep. And they who heard these sayings treasured them in their hearts and did often recite them for the edification of the apostles and disciples who were not present when they were spoken." P159,S3,PP1,PG1765

"Verily, verily, I say to you, he who rules his own self is greater than he who captures a city. Self-mastery is the measure of man's moral nature and the indicator of his spiritual development." P143,S2,PP3,PG1609

"Then Jesus stood up again and continued teaching his apostles: "I am the true vine, and my Father is the husbandman. I am the vine, and you are the branches. And the Father requires of me only that you shall bear much fruit. The vine is pruned only to increase the fruitfulness of its branches. Every branch coming out of me which bears no fruit, the Father will take away. Every branch which bears fruit, the Father will cleanse that it may bear more fruit. Already are you clean through the word I have spoken, but you must continue to be clean. You must abide in me, and I in you; the branch will die if it is separated from the vine. As the branch cannot bear fruit except it abides in the vine, so neither can you yield the fruits of loving service except you abide in me. Remember: I am the real vine, and you are the living branches. He who lives in me, and I in him, will bear much fruit of the spirit and experience the supreme joy of yielding this spiritual harvest. If you will maintain this living spiritual connection with me, you will bear abundant fruit. If you abide in me and my words live in you, you will be able to commune freely with me, and then can my living spirit so infuse you that you may ask whatsoever my spirit wills and do all this with the assurance that the Father will grant us our petition. Herein is the Father glorified: that the vine has many living branches, and that every branch bears much fruit. And when the world sees these fruit-bearing branches—my friends who love one another, even as I have loved them—all men will know that you are truly my disciples." P180,S2,PP1,PG1945

j. *Fruits of the Spirit*

"If, then, my children, you are born of the spirit, you are forever delivered from the self-conscious bondage of a life of self-denial and watchcare over the desires of the flesh, and you are translated into the joyous kingdom of the spirit, whence you spontaneously show forth the fruits of the spirit in your daily lives; and the fruits of the spirit are the essence of the highest type of enjoyable and ennobling self-control, even the heights of terrestrial mortal attainment—true self-mastery." P143,S2,PP8,PG1610

"... "for the fruits of the spirit are love, joy, peace, long-suffering, gentleness, goodness, faith, meekness, and temperance."" P34,S6,PP13,PP381

Who Jesus Was, What He Did, and Excerpts from His Life and Teachings — Chapter 12

"... So does the true believer exist only for the purpose of bearing the fruits of the spirit: to love man as he himself has been loved by God—that we should love one another, even as Jesus has loved us." P180,S2,PP5,PG1946

"... And the fruits of the divine spirit which are yielded in the lives of spirit-born and God-knowing mortals are: loving service, unselfish devotion, courageous loyalty, sincere fairness, enlightened honesty, undying hope, confiding trust, merciful ministry, unfailing goodness, forgiving tolerance, and enduring peace." P193,S2,PP2,PG2054

k. *Examples of Healings*

Healings, or what can happen when a loving, merciful, compassionate Creator Son, working in harmony with the Paradise Father, incarnates on Earth as a human being:

"Jesus had passed the responsibility of this healing decision to the ruling of his Father. Evidently the Father's will interposed no objection, for the words of the Master had scarcely been uttered when the assembly of celestial personalities serving under the command of Jesus' Personalized Thought Adjuster [see the glossary] was mightily astir. The vast retinue descended into the midst of this motley throng of afflicted mortals, and in a moment of time 683 men, women, and children were made whole, were perfectly healed of all their physical diseases and other material disorders. Such a scene was never witnessed on earth before that day, nor since. And for those of us who were present to behold this creative wave of healing, it was indeed a thrilling spectacle."
P145,S3,PP10,PG1633

"While the house was thus thronged with people and entirely surrounded by eager listeners, a man long afflicted with paralysis was carried down from Capernaum on a small couch by his friends. This paralytic had heard that Jesus was about to leave Bethsaida, and having talked with Aaron the stone mason, who had been so recently made whole, he resolved to be carried into Jesus' presence, where he could seek healing. His friends tried to gain entrance to Zebedee's house by both the front and back doors, but too many people were crowded together. But the paralytic refused to accept defeat; he directed his friends to procure ladders by which they ascended to the roof of the room in which Jesus was speaking, and after loosening the tiles, they boldly lowered the sick man on his couch by ropes until the afflicted one rested on the floor immediately in front of the Master. When Jesus saw what they had done, he ceased speaking, while those who were with him in the room marveled at the perseverance of the sick man and his friends. Said the paralytic: "Master, I would not disturb your teaching, but I am determined to be made whole. I am not like those who received healing and immediately forgot your teaching. I would be made whole that I might serve in the kingdom of heaven." Now, notwithstanding that this man's affliction had been brought upon him by his own misspent life, Jesus, seeing his faith, said to the paralytic: "Son, fear not; your sins are forgiven. Your faith shall save you."

When the Pharisees from Jerusalem, together with other scribes and lawyers who sat with them, heard this pronouncement by Jesus, they began to say to themselves: "How dare this man thus speak? Does he not understand that such words are blasphemy? Who can forgive sin but God?" Jesus, perceiving in his spirit that they thus reasoned within their own minds and among themselves, spoke to them, saying: "Why do you so reason in your hearts? Who are you that you sit in judgment over me? What is the difference whether I say to this paralytic, your sins are forgiven, or arise, take up your bed, and walk? But that you who witness all this may finally know that the Son of Man has authority and power on earth to forgive sins, I will say to this afflicted man, Arise, take up your bed, and go to your own house." And when Jesus had thus spoken, the paralytic arose, and as they made way for him, he walked out before them all. And those who saw these things were amazed. Peter dismissed the assemblage, while many prayed and glorified God, confessing that they had never before seen such strange happenings." P148,S9,PP2,PG1666

l. *Miscellaneous Excerpts*

"All down through the ages men have not been unable to comprehend Jesus; they have been afraid to." P156,S2,PP4,PG1736

"The pictures of Jesus have been most unfortunate. These paintings of the Christ have exerted a deleterious influence on youth; the temple merchants would hardly have fled before Jesus if he had been such a man as your artists usually have depicted. His was a dignified manhood; he was good, but natural. Jesus did not pose as a mild, sweet, gentle, and kindly mystic. His teaching was thrillingly dynamic. He not only meant well, but he went about actually doing good." P141,S3,PP6,PG1590

"When the crowd heard these words, they fell to wrangling among themselves. Some said he was mad; some that he had a devil. Others said this was indeed the prophet of Galilee whom the scribes and Pharisees had long sought to kill. Some said the religious authorities were afraid to molest him; others thought that they laid not hands upon him because they had become believers in him. After considerable debate one of the crowd stepped forward and asked Jesus, "Why do the rulers seek to kill you?" And he replied: "The rulers seek to kill me because they resent my teaching about the good news of the kingdom, a gospel that sets men free from the burdensome traditions of a formal religion of ceremonies which these teachers are determined to uphold at any cost. They circumcise in accordance with the law on the Sabbath day, but they would kill me because I once on the Sabbath day set free a man held in the bondage of affliction. They follow after me on the Sabbath to spy on me but would kill me because on another occasion I chose to make a grievously stricken man completely whole on the Sabbath day. They seek to kill me because they well know that, if you honestly believe and dare to accept my teaching, their system of traditional religion will be overthrown, forever destroyed. Thus will they be deprived of authority over that to which they have devoted their lives since they steadfastly refuse to accept this new and more glorious gospel of the kingdom of God. And now do I appeal to every one of you: Judge not according to outward appearances but rather judge by the true spirit of these teachings; judge righteously." P162,S2,PP2,PG1790

"It was also at Jericho, in connection with the discussion of the early religious training of children in habits of divine worship, that Jesus impressed upon his apostles the great value of beauty as an influence leading to the urge to worship, especially with children. The Master by precept and example taught the value of worshiping the Creator in the midst of the natural surroundings of creation. He preferred to commune with the heavenly Father amidst the trees and among the lowly creatures of the natural world. He rejoiced to contemplate the Father through the inspiring spectacle of the starry realms of the Creator Sons." P167,S6,PP5,PG1840

"Jesus spread good cheer everywhere he went. He was full of grace and truth. His associates never ceased to wonder at the gracious words that proceeded out of his mouth. You can cultivate gracefulness, but graciousness is the aroma of friendliness which emanates from a love-saturated soul.

Goodness always compels respect, but when it is devoid of grace, it often repels affection. Goodness is universally attractive only when it is gracious. Goodness is effective only when it is attractive." P171,S7,PP1,PG1874

"Many times has this unreasoning and un-Christlike hatred and persecution of modern Jews terminated in the suffering and death of some innocent and unoffending Jewish individual whose very ancestors, in the times of Jesus, heartily accepted his gospel and presently died unflinchingly for that truth which they so wholeheartedly believed. What a shudder of horror passes over the onlooking celestial beings as they behold the professed followers of Jesus indulge themselves in persecuting, harassing, and even murdering the later-day descendants of Peter, Philip, Matthew, and others of the Palestinian Jews who so gloriously yielded up their lives as the first martyrs of the gospel of the heavenly kingdom!" P175,S2,PP2,PG1909

"Jesus lived a life which is a revelation of man submitted to the Father's will, not an example for any man literally to attempt to follow. This life in the flesh, together with his death on the cross and subsequent resurrection, presently became a new gospel of the ransom which had thus been paid in order to purchase man back from the clutch of the evil one—from the condemnation of an offended God. Nevertheless, even though the gospel did become greatly distorted, it remains a fact that this new message about Jesus carried along with it many of the fundamental truths and teachings of his earlier gospel of the kingdom. And, sooner or later, these concealed truths of the fatherhood of God and the brotherhood of men will emerge to effectually transform the civilization of all mankind." P194,S2,PP8,PG2061

"The teaching regarding Christ's love for children soon put an end to the widespread practice of exposing children to death when they were not wanted, particularly girl babies." P195,S3,PP5,PG2073

"As you view the world, remember that the black patches of evil which you see are shown against a white background of ultimate good. You do not view merely white patches of good which show up miserably against a black background of evil." P195,S5,PP8,PG2076

"You would be neither shocked nor disturbed by some of Jesus' strong pronouncements if you would only remember that he was the world's most wholehearted and devoted religionist. He was a wholly consecrated mortal, unreservedly dedicated to doing his Father's will. Many of his apparently hard sayings were more of a personal confession of faith and a pledge of devotion than commands to his followers. And it was this very singleness of purpose and unselfish devotion that enabled him to effect such extraordinary progress in the conquest of the human mind in one short life. Many of his declarations should be considered as a confession of what he demanded of himself rather than what he required of all his followers. In his devotion to the cause of the kingdom, Jesus burned all bridges behind him; he sacrificed all hindrances to the doing of his Father's will.

"Jesus blessed the poor because they were usually sincere and pious; he condemned the rich because they were usually wanton and irreligious. He would equally condemn the irreligious pauper and commend the consecrated and worshipful man of wealth." P196,S2,PP7,PG2093

"But you should not become discouraged by the apparently slow progress of the kingdom idea on Urantia. Remember that the order of progressive evolution is subjected to sudden and unexpected periodical changes in both the material and the spiritual worlds. The bestowal of Jesus as an incarnated Son was just such a strange and unexpected event in the spiritual life of the world. Neither make the fatal mistake, in looking for the age manifestation of the kingdom, of failing to effect its establishment within your own souls." P170,S4,PP9,PG1863

m. *On Jesus' Promised Return*

"And your record tells the truth when it says that this same Jesus has promised some time to return to the world of his terminal bestowal, the World of the Cross." P119,S8,PP8,PG1319

"Although Jesus referred one phase of the kingdom to the future and did, on numerous occasions, intimate that such an event might appear as a part of a world crisis; and though he did likewise most certainly, on several occasions, definitely promise sometime to return to Urantia, it should be recorded that he never positively linked these two ideas together. He promised a new revelation of the kingdom on earth and at some future time; he also promised sometime to come back to this world in person; but he did not say that these two events were synonymous. From all we know these promises may, or may not, refer to the same event." P170,S4,PP10,PG1863

"We most positively believe that Michael will again come in person to Urantia, but we have not the slightest idea as to when or in what manner he may choose to come. Will his second advent on earth be timed to occur in connection with the terminal judgment of this present age, either with or without the associated appearance of a Magisterial Son? Will he come in connection with the termination of some subsequent Urantian age? Will he come unannounced and as an isolated event? We do not know. Only one thing we are certain of, that is, when he does return, all the world will likely know about it, for he must come as the supreme ruler of a universe and not as the obscure babe of Bethlehem. But if every eye is to behold him, and if only spiritual eyes are to discern his presence, then must his advent be long deferred." P176,S4,PP5,PG1919

n. *Nearing the End of His Earth Life*

"On Sunday the triumphal entry into Jerusalem so overawed the Jewish leaders that they refrained from placing Jesus under arrest. Today, this spectacular cleansing of the temple likewise effectively postponed the Master's apprehension. Day by day the rulers of the Jews were becoming more and more determined to destroy him, but they were distraught by two fears, which conspired to delay the hour of striking. The chief priests and the scribes were unwilling to arrest Jesus in public for fear the multitude might turn upon them in a fury of resentment; they also dreaded the possibility of the Roman guards being called upon to quell a popular uprising." P173,S2,PP1,PG1891

"As Judas approached the home of Caiaphas, he arrived at the final decision to abandon Jesus and his fellow apostles; and having thus made up his mind to desert the cause of the kingdom of heaven, he was determined to secure for himself as much as possible of that honor and glory which he had thought would sometime be his when he first identified himself with Jesus and the new gospel of the kingdom. All of the apostles once shared this ambition with Judas, but as time passed they learned to admire truth and to love Jesus, at least more than did Judas." P177,S4,PP5,PG1925

o. ***The Last Supper***

"They expected the Master to arrive any moment, but they were in a quandary as to whether they should seat themselves or await his coming and depend on him to assign them their places. While they hesitated, Judas stepped over to the seat of honor, at the left of the host, and signified that he intended there to recline as the preferred guest. This act of Judas immediately stirred up a heated dispute among the other apostles. Judas had no sooner seized the seat of honor than John Zebedee laid claim to the next preferred seat, the one on the right of the host. Simon Peter was so enraged at this assumption of choice positions by Judas and John that, as the other angry apostles looked on, he marched clear around the table and took his place on the lowest couch, the end of the seating order and just opposite to that chosen by John Zebedee. Since others had seized the high seats, Peter thought to choose the lowest, and he did this, not merely in protest against the unseemly pride of his brethren, but with the hope that Jesus, when he should come and see him in the place of least honor, would call him up to a higher one, thus displacing one who had presumed to honor himself."

With the highest and lowest positions thus occupied, the rest of the apostles chose places, some near Judas and some near Peter, until all were located. They were seated about the U-shaped table on these reclining divans in the following order: on the right of the Master, John; on the left, Judas, Simon Zelotes, Matthew, James Zebedee, Andrew, the Alpheus twins, Philip, Nathaniel, Thomas, and Simon Peter.

They are gathered together to celebrate, at least in spirit, an institution which antedated even Moses and referred to the times when their fathers were slaves in Egypt. This supper is their last rendezvous with Jesus, and even in such a solemn setting, under the leadership of Judas the apostles are led once more to give way to their old predilection for honor, preference, and personal exaltation.

They were still engaged in voicing angry recriminations when the Master appeared in the doorway, where he hesitated a moment as a look of disappointment slowly crept over his face. Without comment he went to his place, and he did not disturb their seating arrangement.

They were now ready to begin the supper, except that their feet were still unwashed, and they were in anything but a pleasant frame of mind. When the Master arrived, they were still engaged in making uncomplimentary remarks about one another, to say nothing of the thoughts of some who had sufficient emotional control to refrain from publicly expressing their feelings."" P179,S1,PP4,PG1937

"In like manner the Master went around the table, in silence, washing the feet of his twelve apostles, not even passing by Judas." P179,S3,PP7,PG1939

"When I came into this chamber tonight, you were not content proudly to refuse to wash one another's feet, but you must also fall to disputing among yourselves as to who should have the places of honor at my table. Such honors the Pharisees and the children of this world seek, but it should not be so among the ambassadors of the heavenly kingdom. Do you not know that there can be no place of preferment at my table? Do you not understand that I love each of you as I do the others? Do you not know that the place nearest me, as men regard such honors, can mean nothing concerning your standing in the kingdom of heaven ? You know that the kings of the gentiles have lordship over their subjects, while those who exercise this authority are sometimes called benefactors. But it shall not be so in the kingdom of heaven. He who would be great among you, let him become as the younger; while he who would be chief, let him become as one who serves. Who is the greater, he who sits at meat, or he who serves? Is it not commonly regarded that he who sits at meat is the greater? But you will observe that I am among you as one who serves. If you are willing to become fellow servants with me in doing the Father's will, in the kingdom to come you shall sit with me in power, still doing the Father's will in future glory." P179,S3,PP9,PG1940

p. **Last Moments of Freedom**

"After all was still and quiet about the camp, Jesus, taking Peter, James, and John, went a short way up a near-by ravine where he had often before gone to pray and commune. The three apostles could not help recognizing that he was grievously oppressed; never before had they observed their Master to be so heavy-laden and sorrowful. When they arrived at the place of his devotions, he bade the three sit down and watch with him while he went off about a stone's throw to pray. And when he had fallen down on his face, he prayed: "My Father, I came into this world to do your will, and so have I. I know that the hour has come to lay down this life in the flesh, and I do not shrink therefrom, but I would know that it is your will that I drink this cup. Send me the assurance that I will please you in my death even as I have in my life."

The Master remained in a prayerful attitude for a few moments, and then, going over to the three apostles, he found them sound asleep, for their eyes were heavy and they could not remain awake. As Jesus awoke them, he said: "What! can you not watch with me even for one hour? Cannot you see that my soul is exceedingly sorrowful, even to death, and that I crave your companionship?" After the three had aroused from their slumber, the Master again went apart by himself and, falling down on the ground, again prayed: "Father, I know it is possible to avoid this cup—all things are possible with you —but I have come to do your will, and while this is a bitter cup, I would drink it if it is your will." And when he had thus prayed, a mighty angel came down by his side and, speaking to him, touched him and strengthened him.

When Jesus returned to speak with the three apostles, he again found them fast asleep. He awakened them, saying: "In such an hour I need that you should watch and pray with me—all the more do you need to pray that you enter not into temptation—wherefore do you fall asleep when I leave you?"

And then, for a third time, the Master withdrew and prayed: "Father, you see my sleeping apostles; have mercy upon them. The spirit is indeed willing, but the flesh is weak. And now, O Father, if this cup may not pass, then would I drink it. Not my will, but yours, be done." And when he had finished praying, he lay for a moment prostrate on the ground. When he arose and went back to his apostles, once more he found them asleep. He surveyed them and, with a pitying gesture, tenderly said: "Sleep on now and take your rest; the time of decision is past. The hour is now upon us wherein the Son of Man will be betrayed into the hands of his enemies." As he reached down to shake them that he might awaken them, he said: "Arise, let us be going back to the camp, for, behold, he who betrays me is at hand, and the hour has come when my flock shall be scattered. But I have already told you about these things." P182,S3,PP1,PG1968

"The experience of parting with the apostles was a great strain on the human heart of Jesus; this sorrow of love bore down on him and made it more difficult to face such a death as he well knew awaited him. He realized how weak and how ignorant his apostles were, and he dreaded to leave them. He well knew that the time of his departure had come, but his human heart longed to find out whether there might not possibly be some legitimate avenue of escape from this terrible plight of suffering and sorrow. And when it had thus sought escape, and failed, it was willing to drink the cup. The divine mind of Michael knew he had done his best for the twelve apostles; but the human heart of Jesus wished that more might have been done for them before they should be left alone in the world. Jesus' heart was being crushed; he truly loved his brethren. He was isolated from his family in the flesh; one of his chosen associates was betraying him. His father Joseph's people had rejected him and thereby sealed their doom as a people with a special mission on earth. His soul was tortured by baffled love and rejected mercy. It was just one of those awful human moments when everything seems to bear down with crushing cruelty and terrible agony.

Jesus' humanity was not insensible to this situation of private loneliness, public shame, and the appearance of the failure of his cause. All these sentiments bore down on him with indescribable heaviness. In this great sorrow his mind went back to the days of his childhood in Nazareth and to his early work in Galilee. At the time of this great trial there came up in his mind many of those pleasant scenes of his earthly ministry. And it was from these old memories of Nazareth, Capernaum, Mount Hermon, and of the sunrise and sunset on the shimmering Sea of Galilee, that he soothed himself as he made his human heart strong and ready to encounter the traitor who should so soon betray him.

Before Judas and the soldiers arrived, the Master had fully regained his customary poise; the spirit had triumphed over the flesh; faith had asserted itself over all human tendencies to fear or entertain doubt. The supreme test of the full realization of the human nature had been met and acceptably passed. Once more the Son of Man was prepared to face his enemies with equanimity and in the full assurance of his invincibility as a mortal man unreservedly dedicated to the doing of his Father's will."
P182,S3,PP9,PG1969

Chapter 12

9. The Crucifixion

"Shortly after one o'clock, amidst the increasing darkness of the fierce sandstorm, Jesus began to fail in human consciousness. His last words of mercy, forgiveness, and admonition had been spoken. His last wish—concerning the care of his mother—had been expressed. During this hour of approaching death the human mind of Jesus resorted to the repetition of many passages in the Hebrew scriptures, particularly the Psalms. The last conscious thought of the human Jesus was concerned with the repetition in his mind of a portion of the Book of Psalms now known as the twentieth, twenty-first, and twenty-second Psalms. While his lips would often move, he was too weak to utter the words as these passages, which he so well knew by heart, would pass through his mind. Only a few times did those standing by catch some utterance, such as, "I know the Lord will save his anointed," "Your hand shall find out all my enemies," and "My God, my God, why have you forsaken me?" Jesus did not for one moment entertain the slightest doubt that he had lived in accordance with the Father's will; and he never doubted that he was now laying down his life in the flesh in accordance with his Father's will. He did not feel that the Father had forsaken him; he was merely reciting in his vanishing consciousness many Scriptures, among them this twenty-second Psalm, which begins with "My God, my God, why have you forsaken me?" And this happened to be one of the three passages which were spoken with sufficient clearness to be heard by those standing by." P187,S5,PP2,PG2010

"There is great danger of misunderstanding the meaning of numerous sayings and many events associated with the termination of the Master's career in the flesh. The cruel treatment of Jesus by the ignorant servants and the calloused soldiers, the unfair conduct of his trials, and the unfeeling attitude of the professed religious leaders, must not be confused with the fact that Jesus, in patiently submitting to all this suffering and humiliation, was truly doing the will of the Father in Paradise. It was, indeed and in truth, the will of the Father that his Son should drink to the full the cup of mortal experience, from birth to death, but the Father in heaven had nothing whatever to do with instigating the barbarous behavior of those supposedly civilized human beings who so brutally tortured the Master and so horribly heaped successive indignities upon his nonresisting person. These inhuman and shocking experiences which Jesus was called upon to endure in the final hours of his mortal life were not in any sense a part of the divine will of the Father, which his human nature had so triumphantly pledged to carry out at the time of the final surrender of man to God as signified in the threefold prayer which he indited in the garden while his weary apostles slept the sleep of physical exhaustion.

The Father in heaven desired the bestowal Son to finish his earth career *naturally*, just as all mortals must finish up their lives on earth and in the flesh. Ordinary men and women cannot expect to have their last hours on earth and the supervening episode of death made easy by a special dispensation. Accordingly, Jesus elected to lay down his life in the flesh in the manner which was in keeping with the outworking of natural events, and he steadfastly refused to extricate himself from the cruel clutches of a wicked conspiracy of inhuman events which swept on with horrible certainty toward his unbelievable humiliation and ignominious death. And every bit of all this astounding manifestation of hatred and this unprecedented demonstration of cruelty was the work of evil men and wicked mortals. God in heaven did not will it, neither did the archenemies of Jesus dictate it, though they did much to insure that unthinking and evil mortals would thus reject the bestowal Son. Even the father of sin turned his face away from the excruciating horror of the scene of the crucifixion." P183,S1,PP1,PG1971

"The great thing about the death of Jesus, as it is related to the enrichment of human experience and the enlargement of the way of salvation, is not the *fact* of his death but rather the superb manner and the matchless spirit in which he met death." P188,S4,PP12,PG2017

"It is a fact that Urantia has become known among other neighboring inhabited planets as the "World of the Cross."" P188,S4,PP1,PG2016

r. **The Resurrection**

"The mortals of the realms will arise in the morning of the resurrection with the same type of transition or morontia body that Jesus had when he arose from the tomb on this Sunday morning. These bodies do not have circulating blood, and such beings do not partake of ordinary material food; nevertheless, these morontia forms are *real*. When the various believers saw Jesus after his resurrection, they really saw him; they were not the self-deceived victims of visions or hallucinations." P190,PP3,PG2029

"After the resurrected Jesus emerged from his burial tomb, the body of flesh in which he had lived and wrought on earth for almost thirty-six years was still lying there in the sepulchre niche, undisturbed and wrapped in the linen sheet, just as it had been laid to rest by Joseph and his associates on Friday afternoon. Neither was the stone before the entrance of the tomb in any way disturbed; the seal of Pilate was still unbroken; the soldiers were still on guard. The temple guards had been on continuous duty; the Roman guard had been changed at midnight. None of these watchers suspected that the object of their vigil had risen to a new and higher form of existence, and that the body which they were guarding was now a discarded outer covering which had no further connection with the delivered and resurrected morontia personality of Jesus." P189,S1,PP2,PG2021

Jesus in morontia form had left his body; then, certain celestial personalities obtained permission to take his body and speed up its material dissolution:

"As they made ready to remove the body of Jesus from the tomb preparatory to according it the dignified and reverent disposal of near-instantaneous dissolution, it was assigned the secondary Urantia midwayers to roll away the stones from the entrance of the tomb. The larger of these two stones was a huge circular affair, much like a millstone, and it moved in a groove chiseled out of the rock, so that it could be rolled back and forth to open or close the tomb. When the watching Jewish guards and the Roman soldiers, in the dim light of the morning, saw this huge stone begin to roll away from the entrance of the tomb, apparently of its own accord—without any visible means to account for such motion—they were seized with fear and panic, and they fled in haste from the scene...." P189,S2,PP4,PG2023

"The mortal remains of Jesus underwent the same natural process of elemental disintegration as characterizes all human bodies on earth except that, in point of time, this natural mode of dissolution was greatly accelerated, hastened to that point where it became well-nigh instantaneous." P189,S2,PP8,PG2024

Then, until his ascension to the Father, Jesus made appearances in morontia form to various human believers.

"By the aid of certain morontia auxiliary personalities, the morontia form can be made at one time as of the spirit so that it can become indifferent to ordinary matter, while at another time it can become discernible and contactable to material beings, such as the mortals of the realm." P189,S2,PP3,PG2023

"From the time of the morontia resurrection until the hour of his spirit ascension on high, Jesus made nineteen separate appearances in visible form to his believers on earth. He did not appear to his enemies nor to those who could not make spiritual use of his manifestation in visible form. His first appearance was to the five women at the tomb; his second, to Mary Magdalene, also at the tomb." P190,S2,PP1,PG2031

"These human eyes were enabled to see the morontia form of Jesus because of the special ministry of the transformers and the midwayers in association with certain of the morontia personalities then accompanying Jesus.

As Mary [Magdalene] sought to embrace his feet, Jesus said: "Touch me not, Mary, for I am not as you knew me in the flesh. In this form will I tarry with you for a season before I ascend to the Father. But go, all of you, now and tell my apostles— and Peter—that I have risen, and that you have talked with me." P189,S4,PP11,PG2027

s. *Pentecost and the Bestowal of the Spirit of Truth*

"Many queer and strange teachings became associated with the early narratives of the day of Pentecost. In subsequent times the events of this day, on which the Spirit of Truth, the new teacher, came to dwell with mankind, have become confused with the foolish outbreaks of rampant emotionalism. The chief mission of this outpoured spirit of the Father and the Son is to teach men about the truths of the Father's love and the Son's mercy. These are the truths of divinity which men can comprehend more fully than all the other divine traits of character. The Spirit of Truth is concerned primarily with the revelation of the Father's spirit nature and the Son's moral character. The Creator Son, in the flesh, revealed God to men; the Spirit of Truth, in the heart, reveals the Creator Son to men. When man yields the "fruits of the spirit" in his life, he is simply showing forth the traits which the Master manifested in his own earthly life. When Jesus was on earth, he lived his life as one personality—Jesus of Nazareth. As the indwelling spirit of the "new teacher," the Master has, since Pentecost, been able to live his life anew in the experience of every truth-taught believer." P194,S3,PP1,PG2062

"The bestowal of the Spirit of Truth was independent of all forms, ceremonies, sacred places, and special behavior by those who received the fullness of its manifestation. When the spirit came upon those assembled in the upper chamber, they were simply sitting there, having just been engaged in silent prayer. The spirit was bestowed in the country as well as in the city. It was not necessary for the apostles to go apart to a lonely place for years of solitary meditation in order to receive the spirit. For all time, Pentecost disassociates the idea of spiritual experience from the notion of especially favorable environments." P194,S3,PP10,PG2064

"Pentecost was the call to spiritual unity among gospel believers. When the spirit descended on the disciples at Jerusalem, the same thing happened in Philadelphia, Alexandria, and at all other places where true believers dwelt. It was literally true that "there was but one heart and soul among the multitude of the believers." The religion of Jesus is the most powerful unifying influence the world has ever known." P194,S3,PP17,PG2065

"If religion is an opiate to the people, it is not the religion of Jesus. On the cross he refused to drink the deadening drug, and his spirit, poured out upon all flesh, is a mighty world influence which leads man upward and urges him onward. The spiritual forward urge is the most powerful driving force present in this world; the truth-learning believer is the one progressive and aggressive soul on earth." P194,S3,PP4,PG2063

t. *Persecution*

"Stephen and his Greek associate began to preach more as Jesus taught, and this brought them into immediate conflict with the Jewish rulers. In one of Stephen's public sermons, when he reached the objectionable part of the discourse, they dispensed with all formalities of trial and proceeded to stone him to death on the spot." P194,S4,PP11,PG2068

u. *The Fate of The Apostles*

Andrew:

"When the later persecutions finally scattered the apostles from Jerusalem, Andrew journeyed through Armenia, Asia Minor, and Macedonia and, after bringing many thousands into the kingdom, was finally apprehended and crucified in Patrae in Achaia. It was two full days before this robust man expired on the cross, and throughout these tragic hours he continued effectively to proclaim the glad tidings of the salvation of the kingdom of heaven." P139,S1,PP12,PG1550

Peter:

"Peter's wife was a very able woman. For years she labored acceptably as a member of the women's corps, and when Peter was driven out of Jerusalem, she accompanied him upon all his journeys to the churches as well as on all his missionary excursions. And the day her illustrious husband yielded up his life, she was thrown to the wild beasts in the arena at Rome.

And so this man Peter, an intimate of Jesus, one of the inner circle, went forth from Jerusalem proclaiming the glad tidings of the kingdom with power and glory until the fullness of his ministry had been accomplished; and he regarded himself as the recipient of high honors when his captors informed him that he must die as his Master had died—on the cross. And thus was Simon Peter crucified in Rome." P139,S2,PP14,PG1552 [Andrew and Simon Peter were brothers.]

James:

"James lived his life to the full, and when the end came, he bore himself with such grace and fortitude that even his accuser and informer, who attended his trial and execution, was so touched that he rushed away from the scene of James' death to join himself to the disciples of Jesus." P139,S3,PP9,PG1553

John:

"When in temporary exile on Patmos, John wrote the Book of Revelation, which you now have in greatly abridged and distorted form. This Book of Revelation contains the surviving fragments of a great revelation, large portions of which were lost, other portions of which were removed, subsequent to John's writing. It is preserved in only fragmentary and adulterated form.

John traveled much, labored incessantly, and after becoming bishop of the Asia churches, settled down at Ephesus. He directed his associate, Nathan, in the writing of the so-called "Gospel according to John," at Ephesus, when he was ninety-nine years old. Of all the twelve apostles, John Zebedee eventually became the outstanding theologian. He died a natural death at Ephesus in A.D. 103 when he was one hundred and one years of age." P139,S4,PP14,PG1555 [James and John Zebedee were brothers.]

Phillip:

"Philip's wife, who was an efficient member of the women's corps, became actively associated with her husband in his evangelistic work after their flight from the Jerusalem persecutions. His wife was a fearless woman. She stood at the foot of Philip's cross encouraging him to proclaim the glad tidings even to his murderers, and when his strength failed, she began the recital of the story of salvation by faith in Jesus and was silenced only when the irate Jews rushed upon her and stoned her to death. Their eldest daughter, Leah, continued their work, later on becoming the renowned prophetess of Hierapolis.

Philip, the onetime steward of the twelve, was a mighty man in the kingdom, winning souls wherever he went; and he was finally crucified for his faith and buried at Hierapolis." P139,S5,PP11,PG1557

Nathaniel:

"Nathaniel's father (Bartholomew) died shortly after Pentecost, after which this apostle went into Mesopotamia and India proclaiming the glad tidings of the kingdom and baptizing believers. His brethren never knew what became of their onetime philosopher, poet, and humorist. But he also was a great man in the kingdom and did much to spread his Master's teachings, even though he did not participate in the organization of the subsequent Christian church. Nathaniel died in India." P139,S6,PP9,PG1559

Matthew:

"When these persecutions caused the believers to forsake Jerusalem, Matthew journeyed north, preaching the gospel of the kingdom and baptizing believers. He was lost to the knowledge of his former apostolic associates, but on he went, preaching and baptizing, through Syria, Cappadocia, Galatia, Bithynia, and Thrace. And it was in Thrace, at Lysimachia, that certain unbelieving Jews conspired with the Roman soldiers to encompass his death. And this regenerated publican died triumphant in the faith of a salvation he had so surely learned from the teachings of the Master during his recent sojourn on earth." P139,S7,PP10,PG1560

Thomas:

"Thomas had a trying time during the days of the trial and crucifixion. He was for a season in the depths of despair, but he rallied his courage, stuck to the apostles, and was present with them to welcome Jesus on the Sea of Galilee. For a while he succumbed to his doubting depression but eventually rallied his faith and courage. He gave wise counsel to the apostles after Pentecost and, when persecution scattered the believers, went to Cyprus, Crete, the North African coast, and Sicily, preaching the glad tidings of the kingdom and baptizing believers. And Thomas continued preaching and baptizing until he was apprehended by the agents of the Roman government and was put to death in Malta. Just a few weeks before his death he had begun the writing of the life and teachings of Jesus." P139,S8,PP13,PG1563

James and Judas Alpheus:

"The twins served faithfully until the end, until the dark days of trial, crucifixion, and despair. They never lost their heart faith in Jesus, and (save John) they were the first to believe in his resurrection. But they could not comprehend the establishment of the kingdom. Soon after their Master was crucified, they returned to their families and nets; their work was done. They had not the ability to go on in the more complex battles of the kingdom. But they lived and died conscious of having been honored and blessed with four years of close and personal association with a Son of God, the sovereign maker of a universe." P139,S9&10,PP11,PG1564

Simon Zelotes:

"He went to Alexandria and, after working up the Nile, penetrated into the heart of Africa, everywhere preaching the gospel of Jesus and baptizing believers. Thus he labored until he was an old man and feeble. And he died and was buried in the heart of Africa." P139,S11,PP11,PG1565

Judas Iscariot:

"When the sordid and sinful business was all over, this renegade mortal, who thought lightly of selling his friend for thirty pieces of silver to satisfy his long-nursed craving for revenge, rushed out and committed the final act in the drama of fleeing from the realities of mortal existence—suicide.

The eleven apostles were horrified, stunned. Jesus regarded the betrayer only with pity. The worlds have found it difficult to forgive Judas, and his name has become eschewed throughout a far-flung universe." P139,S12,PP13,PG1567

Chapter 12

GLOSSARY

Adams and Eves
: The Material Sons and Daughters, who function as biologic uplifters for evolutionary planets. Here on earth they defaulted, and only partly accomplished their mission.

Adam
: See Adam and Eve.

Adjuster
: See Thought Adjuster.

Adjutant Mind Spirits
: See Seven Adjutant Mind Spirits.

Ancients of Days
: Superuniverse-level adjudicators or judges.

Angels
: See seraphim.

Architecturalized Spheres
: Material spheres in the universe that are directly created, rather than being created through evolution.

Ascending Sons of God
: Humans and other universe inhabitants who learn, grow, and progress upward and inward to the Paradise Father.

Avonal Sons
: Sons of God from Paradise; they are children of The Eternal Son and The Infinite Spirit.

Bestowal Son
: A gift to an evolving planet consisting of a Paradise Son of God incarnated as a mortal of that planet, providing spiritual uplift for the mortal races. Their lives are an incarnation of Paradise truth, resulting in a "new and living way" and resulting in the outpouring of the Spirit of Truth. They are Avonal Sons, except once in each local universe when the Creator Son fulfills this role.

Caligastia
: Our Planetary Prince, our spiritual planetary administrator, a Lanonandek Son, who joined a rebellion against God about 200,000 years ago, causing negative impact to our planetary development and progression.

Caligastia One Hundred
A specially materialized corps of male and female assistants to the Planetary Prince, not created through evolution, and having "superhuman" properties.

Central Universe
A perfect, eternal, divine, harmonious, and beautiful central universe, around which seven huge evolutionary superuniverses exist.

Cherubim
Along with Sanobim are "... the faithful and efficient aids of the seraphic ministers ..." P38,S7,PP3,PG422

Christ Michael
Michael of Nebadon, our local universe Creator Son, incarnated here as Jesus Christ, also called Christ Michael.

Constellation
A universe administrative unit consisting of 100 systems; each system contains, when mature, 1,000 inhabited planets.

Creative Daughter of the Infinite Spirit
See Divine Minister of Salvington.

Creative Spirit
See Divine Minister of Salvington.

Creator Sons
In conjunction with daughters of the Infinite Spirit, create local universes, including the physical realms and the various inhabitants. Creator Sons result from the Paradise Father and the Paradise Son sharing a certain type of creative thought. Creator Sons are of the order of Michaels, our local universe is named Nebadon, therefore our Creator Son is called Michael of Nebadon, and He incarnated here as Jesus Christ.

Dalamatia
The material, planetary headquarters and teaching city administered by the Planetary Prince and his staff for 300,000 years; came to an end along with the rebellion about 200,000 years ago.

Daligastia
Our Planetary Prince's assistant, a Lanonandek Son, who also joined the rebellion against God.

Daughter of the Infinite Spirit
Refers to an offspring, such as an angel, coming from the Infinite Spirit. See also Divine Minister of Salvington.

Descending Sons of God
"Descending orders of sonship include personalities who are of direct and divine creation." P20,PP2,PG223 "All descending Sons of God have high and divine origins. They are dedicated to the descending ministry of service on the worlds and systems of time and space ..." P20,S1,PP1,PG223

Divinington
: One of the seven sacred worlds of the Father, near Paradise. It is a Paradise rendezvous for Thought Adjusters, and is a "personal-communion sphere of the Paradise Father, ..." P13,S1,PP4,PG144

Divine Minister of Salvington
: One of the names for the local universe representative of the Paradise Infinite Spirit, also known as the local universe Mother Spirit or Creative Spirit. Is coordinate, along with a Creator Son, in creation of a local universe. See also Holy Spirit.

Edentia
: The headquarters sphere of the constellation to which our system belongs.

Era of Light and Life
: The destiny of every evolutionary planet. The planet goes positive. The glory and goodness of God are manifested in the human realm.

Eternal Son
: The Second Source and Center, one of the Paradise Trinity.

Eve
: See Adam and Eve.

First Cause
: See First Source and Center.

First Source and Center
: The Universal or Paradise Father, one of the Paradise Trinity.

Fusion
: When an Adjuster-indwelt ascending son or daughter of God is ready to make, and makes, a final and irrevocable decision to do the will of God, it is confirmed by the fusion of that personality with the indwelling fragment of God.

Gabriel
: Gabriel is an order of being called a Bright and Morning Star, and there is only one in each local universe. They come from a union of the local universe Creator Son and the local universe Creative Mother Spirit, and act as chief executives for Creator Sons in local universes.

Garden of Eden
: Now submerged by geologic processes, but previously located on the eastern shore of the Mediterranean Sea, the actual dwelling place of our planetary Adam and Eve when they were here about 38,000 years ago.

God the Father
: See First Source and Center, a member of the Paradise Trinity.

God the Supreme
: An evolving or evolutionary aspect of God, in which the material, spiritual, and in-between realms are coordinated, and one which finite (time-space) universe inhabitants can add to.

Grand Universe
: The seven evolutionary superuniverses and the eternal central universe.

Havona
: The name of the eternal central universe.

Holy Spirit
: Is the ministering Spirit of the local universe representative of the Paradise Infinite Spirit, who is known as the local universe Divine Minister, Mother Spirit, or Creative Spirit.

Immanuel
: Is a Paradise Trinity ambassador residing in our local universe of Nebadon, and is a Paradise Trinity advisor, and counselor upon request, to our local universe Creator Son, Michael.

Infinite Spirit
: The Third Source and Center, one of the Paradise Trinity. Is omnipresent throughout the universe of universes.

Isle of Paradise
: The gravity center of the universe of universes, the dwelling place of God, the eternal Isle of Light and Life. Time and space emanate from it.

Jerusem
: Our local system headquarters sphere.

Lanonandek Sons
: An order of local universe descending Sons of God.

Life Carrier Sons
: An order of local universe descending Sons of God.

Local Universe
: A universe created by a Creator Son and a Daughter of the Infinite Spirit. Consists of 100 constellations; each constellation consists of 100 systems; each system has about 1,000 inhabited planets when mature.

Local Universe Divine Minister
: See Divine Minister of Salvington and Holy Spirit.

Local Universe Mother Spirit
: See Divine Minister of Salvington.

Lucifer
: Our previous System Sovereign, a Lanonandek Son, who along with Satan instigated a rebellion against God in our local system.

Machiventa Melchizedek
: A local universe Melchizedek Son of God, who incarnated in human form as a full grown male in 1,973 B.C.. His was an emergency mission to keep truths about God alive and active on the planet. He is mentioned in the Bible as Melchizedek.

Magisterial Sons
: Paradise representatives; see Avonal Sons. Magisterial Sons are Avonal sons, just as Creator Sons are Michael Sons.

Major Sector
> One hundred minor sectors comprise a major sector, and 10 major sectors comprise one of the seven superuniverses.

Mansion Worlds
> There are fifty-six worlds encircling Jerusem, the headquarters sphere of our local system. These consist of seven primary worlds, each with seven satellites. The seven satellites that encircle world number one are the mansion worlds, the worlds where we are resurrected and begin our post-planetary progression upward and inward toward God.

Mansonia Number One, Two, etc.
> Are the names of the individual mansion worlds.

Master Universe
> Includes the eternal central universe; the surrounding seven evolutionary superuniverses; and the outer, currently mobilizing areas of outer space.

Material Son and Daughter
> The Adams and Eves, who function as biologic uplifters for evolutionary planets. Here, they defaulted, and only partly accomplished their mission.

Melchizedek Sons
> An order of local universe Sons of God, who do emergency services, among other things.

Michael
> See Michael of Nebadon

Michael of Nebadon
> Creator Sons are of the order of Michaels, our local universe is named Nebadon; therefore, our local universe Creator Son is called Michael of Nebadon. In conjunction with a Daughter of the Infinite Spirit, creates a local universe, including the physical realms and the various inhabitants. Our Creator Son incarnated here as Jesus Christ, our Bestowal Son. Also called Michael or Christ Michael.

Midwayers
> "... unique beings existing on a life-functioning level about midway between those of the mortals of the realms and of the angelic orders; hence are they called midway creatures." P77,PP1,PG855 They are created and live on the planets.

Minor Sector
> One hundred local universes comprise a minor sector.

Monitor
> See Mystery Monitor or Thought Adjuster.

Morontia
> "... a vast level intervening between the material and the spiritual. It may designate personal or impersonal realities, living or nonliving energies. The warp of morontia is spiritual; its woof is physical." FOREWORD,SV,PP8,PG9

Morontial
> Having to do with morontia.

Most Highs
: Local universe sons of God who act as constellation Fathers, among other duties. Most Highs rule in the affairs of humans, to achieve the greatest good for the greatest number of people for the greatest length of time.

Mother Spirit
: One of the names for the local universe representative of the Paradise Infinite Spirit, also known as the local universe Divine Minister, or Creative Spirit. Is coordinate in creation of a local universe.

Mystery Monitor
: The fragment of God that indwells the human mind, leading us Godward.

Nebadon
: The name of our local universe.

Nodites
: A grouping of people living on Earth, outside the Garden of Eden, in the times of Adam and Eve.

Orvonton
: The name of our evolutionary superuniverse, which is one of seven. Will contain one trillion inhabited planets, approximately, when mature.

Paradise
: A material higher than us lowly creatures can imagine; beauty and wonders beyond comprehension; see Isle of Paradise. Interestingly, the smallest units of organized energy out here in the time space creations, ultimatons, have Paradise as their nucleus.

Paradise Corps of the Finality
: We, and other ascending daughters and sons of God, progress upward and inward all the way to the Paradise Father. After achieving this, which takes a really long time, we go out to serve in the universes of time as the Paradise Corps of the Finality.

Paradise Creator Son
: See Creator Son. Creator Sons hail from Paradise.

Paradise Father
: The First Source and Center, one of the Paradise Trinity.

Paradise Sons
: Descending Sons of Paradise origin.

Paradise Trinity
: The combination of the original, eternal, Father, Son, and Spirit.

Pentecost
: The time when the Bestowal Son's (Jesus') Spirit of Truth was poured out on the flesh.

Personalized Thought Adjuster
: A Thought Adjuster that through certain types of special service has become a person, that has become personalized. Otherwise, thought adjusters are pre-personal fragments of God.

Planetary Prince
Caligastia, our Planetary Prince, was our spiritual planetary administrator, a Lanonandek Son, who joined a rebellion against God about 200,000 years ago, causing negative impact to our planetary development and progression.

Salvington
Headquarters of our local universe.

Sanobim
Along with Cherubim are "... the faithful and efficient aids of the seraphic ministers ..." P39,S7,PP3,PG422

Second Source and Center
The Second Source and Center, the Eternal Son, one of the Paradise Trinity.

Seraphim
Angels, unseen friends who are ministering spirits. There are many types and functions. The lower orders are only slightly higher than humans. They are daughters of the local universe Creative Mother Spirit.

Satan
Lucifer's first lieutenant or first assistant, also a Lanonandek Son, who joined fully into Lucifer's rebellion against God.

Satania
The name of our local system, in which there are 619 inhabited planets. Urantia is the 606th planet of the 619.

Seven Adjutant Mind-spirits
Mind channels or circuits bestowed by the local universe Divine Minister or Mother Spirit. They are intuition, understanding, courage, knowledge, and counsel, worship, and wisdom. The first five function in animals, all seven function in humans.

Son of Man
What Jesus called himself during the first three years of his ministry as a teacher and healer.

Son of God
What Jesus called himself in the last year of his ministry.

Sonarington
Is a sacred sphere of the Father very close to Paradise.

Spirit of Truth
The bestowed Spirit of Truth that has been poured out upon the flesh. It is the combined spirit of the Universe Father and the Creator Son, but is generally regarded as the Spirit of the local universe Creator Son.

Superuniverse
One of seven evolutionary universes around the eternal central universe of creation.

Supreme Being
See God the Supreme for a basic definition. However, *The Urantia Book* does portray some differences between God the Supreme, the Almighty Supreme, and the Supreme Being.

System
: An administrative unit containing about 1000 inhabited planets when mature.

System Sovereign
: The spiritual chief administrative officer or ruler of a system. Typically are local universe Lanonandek Sons.

Third Source and Center
: The Third Source and Center, the Paradise Infinite Spirit, one of the Paradise Trinity.

Thought Adjuster
: The fragment of the Heavenly Father that indwells the human mind. See Mystery Monitor.

Trinity
: See Paradise Trinity.

Trinity Teacher Sons
: Are divine Sons of the Paradise Trinity

Universal Father
: The Universal or Paradise Father, one of the Paradise Trinity.

Universe Mother Spirit
: See local universe Divine minister.

Urantia
: The name of our planet.

Uversa
: The headquarters of our superuniverse.

Vorondadek Sons
: An order of local universe Sons of God.

BOOK ORDER FORM

Orders available by postal mail only at the time of publication.

Send order to: White Egret Publications
251 F Street
Arcata, CA 95521
Telephone (707) 822-2577

An Introduction to the Urantia Revelation, by David Bradley, Second Edition, 2002

    No. of books ordered: _____

    Price: $14.95 ea. _____

7.25% tax if CA address ($1.08ea) _____

    $2.00 ea. Shipping _____

    Total: $ _____

Please enclose check or money order for the total amount.

Name (please print):_____

Street Address: _____

City:_____ State:_____ Zip:_____ - _____

If in California, please include County:_____

I appreciate any comments you have about this book. Please mail comments to: David Bradley, White Egret Publications, 251 F Street, Arcata, CA 95521.
COMMENTS: _____

_____

_____

_____

_____

_____

_____

_____